REED CONCISE GUIDE

Ken Stepnell

First published in 2015 by Reed New Holland Publishers Pty Ltd
London • Sydney • Auckland

The Chandlery, 50 Westminster Bridge Road, London SE1 7QY, UK
1/66 Gibbes Street, Chatswood, NSW 2067, Australia
5/39 Woodside Avenue, Northcote, Auckland 0627, New Zealand

www.newhollandpublishers.com

Copyright © 2015 Reed New Holland Publishers Pty Ltd
Copyright © 2015 in text: Ken Stepnell
Copyright © 2015 in photographs: Ken Stepnell and other photographers as credited

All rights reserved. No part of this publication may be reproduced, stored in a retrieval system or transmitted, in any form or by any means, electronic, mechanical, photocopying, recording or otherwise, without the prior written permission of the publishers and copyright holders.

A record of this book is held at the British Library and the National Library of Australia.

ISBN 978 1 92151 753 2

Managing Director: Fiona Schultz
Publisher and Project Editor: Simon Papps
Designer: Thomas Casey
Production Director: Olga Dementiev
Printer: Toppan Leefung Printing Ltd

All images by Ken Stepnell except for the following: Dreamstime (front cover, back cover, pages 1, 6, 13, 18, 22, 23 below, 25, 30, 32, 35, 38, 40, 46, 47 above, 50 below, 53 both images, 54 above, 55 above, 61, 65, 79, 80, 81, 83, 85, 90, 94, 95, 120 both images, 121, 126 above, 150, 157 below, 168 above, 169 below, 170, 177, 180, 183 and 184); and Simon Papps (pages 58 and 86)

10 9 8 7 6 5 4 3 2

Keep up with New Holland Publishers on Facebook
www.facebook.com/NewHollandPublishers

CONTENTS

Introduction 4

Bird families

CASUARIIDAE Cassowary 14
DROMAIIDAE Emu 15
ANSERANATIDAE Magpie goose 16
ANATIDAE Wildfowl 17
MEGAPODIIDAE Megapodes 29
PODICIPEDIDAE Grebes 31
SPHENISCIDAE Penguins 33
DIOMEDEIDAE Albatrosses 34
PROCELLARIIDAE Shearwaters 36
HYDROBATIDAE Storm-petrels 37

Family	Common name	Page
SULIDAE	Gannets	38
PHALACROCORACIDAE	Cormorants	39
ANHINGIDAE	Darters	40
PELECANIDAE	Pelicans	41
ARDEIDAE	Herons and egrets	42
THRESKIORNITHIDAE	Ibises and spoonbills	48
CICONIIDAE	Storks	51
ACCIPITRIDAE	Hawks and allies	52
FALCONIDAE	Falcons	54
OTIDIDAE	Bustards	56
TURNICIDAE	Buttonquails	57
RALLIDAE	Rails	58
GRUIDAE	Cranes	61
BURHINIDAE	Stone-curlews	62
RECURVIROSTRIDAE	Stilts and oystercatchers	63
CHARADRIIDAE	Plovers	65
LARIDAE	Gulls and terns	70
COLUMBIDAE	Pigeons and doves	75
CUCULIDAE	Cuckoos	81
TYTONIDAE	Barn owls	82
STRIGIDAE	Typical owls	83
PODARGIDAE	Frogmouths	84
APODIDAE	Swifts	85

ALCEDINIDAE Kingfishers	86
MEROPIDAE Bee-eaters	90
CACATUIDAE Cockatoos	91
PSITTACULIDAE Parrots	100
MENURIDAE Lyrebirds	125
PTILONORHYNCHIDAE Bowerbirds	126
CLIMACTERIDAE Treecreepers	129
MALURIDAE Fairy-wrens	131
MELIPHAGIDAE Honeyeaters	132
DASYORNITHIDAE Bristlebirds	147
PARDALOTIDAE Pardalotes	148
ACANTHIZIDAE Scrubwrens and thornbills	150
POMATOSTOMIDAE Babblers	156
ARTAMIDAE Woodswallows	157
CRACTICIDAE Butcherbirds, magpie and currawongs	159
CAMPEPHAGIDAE Cuckooshrikes	162
PACHYCEPHALIDAE Shrike-thrushes and whistlers	163
ORIOLIDAE Orioles	166
RHIPIDURIDAE Fantails	168
MONARCHIDAE Monarchs	170
CORVIDAE Crows	172
PETROICIDAE Australasian robins	173
HIRUNDINIDAE Swallows	177

ACROCEPHALIDAE Reed-warblers	178
CISTICOLIDAE Cisticolas	179
ZOSTEROPIDAE Silvereye	180
TURDIDAE Thrushes	181
DICAEIDAE Mistletoebird	182
ESTRILDIDAE Finches	183
Further reading	186
Glossary	186
Index	188

INTRODUCTION

Australian birds

Nearly 900 species of birds have been recorded in Australia. About a quarter of these are rare visitors to our shores, while a small percentage of the remainder migrate here to nest or visit during their off-season after breeding in other lands, including a wide variety of shorebirds and seabirds. Bird families such as wildfowl, shorebirds, raptors, kingfishers, cuckoos, parrots and honeyeaters are particularly well represented in Australia. About 700 bird species breed on the mainland (including Tasmania) and the country's relatively long-standing geographical isolation has facilitated the evolution of a large number of endemic species, including many types of parrot, honeyeater, fairy-wren, thornbill and whistler. In total nearly half of Australia's breeding birds are endemic species which breed nowhere else on earth.

Nesting

Each species must have suitable conditions in which to nest according to their adaptations. Some have evolved to survive in the dry desert, others in rainforest regions. The rhythm of the season will control the breeding times for many of the Australian bird species, and adequate supply of food for both adults and young will determine their instinct to lay more than one clutch of eggs. Insect-eating birds like fantails, fairy-wrens, magpies and others will often nest twice, and sometimes more, if breeding conditions are

Introduction

favourable. On the other hand, it is uncommon for seed-eating birds like parrots to nest more than once in a season due to restrictions on the abundance of food. Experts believe the number of eggs laid is also dependent upon the food supply. Birds such as Australian Gannet and Short-tailed Shearwater only lay one egg each breeding season, while the likes of emus and ducks often lay up to ten or more eggs.

The style of nest varies considerably. Small birds like the fantails, whistlers and honeyeaters use grass, fibre, or cobweb for nest-building. Crows and magpies will use small sticks and a lining of down and feathers. Birds such as kingfishers and parrots tend to use a hollow in a tree as a nest. Shearwaters use a burrow and also nest in colonies like many other seabirds and waterbirds. Birds such as White-winged Chough, Fairy Martin, Welcome Swallow and Magpie-lark (also known as the 'mudlark') build a nest of mud, while the Australian Gannet builds a nest of guano and small debris on the ground.

Undoubtedly the strangest nests of all are those of megapodes such as the Malleefowl. The male uses his strong feet to scrape up a large mound composed of debris, sand and other material from the forest floor. A chamber is prepared for the female to lay up to 30 eggs. Incubation takes around 50 days, during which time the male tends the nest and ensures that the temperature is maintained at a steady 33°C. When hatched the chicks work their way to the surface and are totally independent from the parents.

In most othe cases, though, either one or both of parents perform the duties of feeding the chicks and keeping them warm and safe until they leave the nest. The young of birds such as plovers and wildfowl also leave the nest almost immediatedly but are still looked after by the parents.

The cuckoos are an interesting case as most species lay their eggs in the nests of other birds – a behaviour known as brood-parasitism. Small cuckoo species lay in the open cupped nests of birds like fantails, larger species such as Channel-billed Cuckoo use magpies or currawongs. The host parents hatch the cuckoo egg and when the young cuckoo is big enough it pushes the other chicks from the nest. The unsuspecting parents just carry on feeding the cuckoo until it fledges.

Migration

Migration is one of the most fascinating aspects of ornithology. A large percentage of Australian birds have some form of migration during the non-breeding season. Flame Robins move down from the high country each autumn to winter on the open lowlands and plains – this is known as 'altitudinal migration'. The Double-banded Plover makes an unusual east-west movement between Australia and New Zealand – this is called 'Trans-Tasman migration'. Some species, such as Pallid Cuckoo and Sacred Kingfisher, move northwards each autumn. Seabirds such as the Short-tailed Shearwater fly a circuit around the extremities of the Pacific Ocean each year and then with precision timing arrive back in Australia to breed. However, perhaps the most amazing migration feats performed by our birds are those made by the Asian-breeding swifts and shorebirds. These birds travel thousands of kilometres each year, southwards during

Introduction

the spring and then northwards during the late summer and autumn. The latter migration takes the birds to their nesting and breeding grounds in Asia, in some cases as far north as the Arctic Circle.

Threats

It is unfortunate that today the populations of many of bird species have declined dramatically, often as a direct result of human activities, including loss of habitat, hunting for food and feathers, trapping for the cagebird trade and predation by introduced species such as foxes. Even small birds that nest a few metres off the ground are easy prey for foxes and feral cats.

The King Island Emu, Kangaroo Island Emu and Paradise Parrot have already been lost, and others, such as the Orange-bellied Parrot and Regent Honeyeater, are listed as 'critically endangered' by BirdLife International.

Even in today's world of great scientific knowledge and advancement, far too little is known about the habits of our birds. Comparatively few life studies have been carried out on Australia's native birds. The banding of many species has given a much-needed insight into their movements, in particular those of migrant birds, and also some new knowledge about their feeding habits. But there is still much work to be done.

Successes

Not all changes made by humans have been bad for the bird populations. Some species, like the grain-eating Galahs and other cockatoos and parrots, together with species such as Magpie-larks, have benefitted from land clearance. These and many more species have been able to expand their range due to habitat changes caused by humans, and they have also benefitted from bores with abundant water at their disposal. Some birds, such as various species of lorikeets, have become so successful that they now pose a problem with orchid- and grape-growers. Some species of honeyeaters have become a familar sight in many suburban gardens, encouraged by the proliferation of grevillea and some varieties of flowering gum which are popular with gardeners, sipping the nectar of these plants with their long, brush-tipped tongues. And spectacular birds such as cockatoos are a familar sight in many gardens, especially when the banksia has cones; with their strong bill they are able to crack open the cone, standing on one foot, using the other foot like a hand to place the cone in the correct position.

Introduction

The species in this book

In this book I have tried to represent a good selection of more than 200 of the bird species found in Australia, and many of these birds are well known to people (for a fully comprehensive title on the subject the *Slater Field Guide to Australian Birds* is an excellent choice). This book has attempted to focus on the most common and widespread species which are likely to be encountered in Australia, while there are also accounts for some of the rarer and more spectacular species such as Southern Cassowary. Each account contains information which is important for identification, including size, field markings, behaviour, habitat, range and voice. While coverage cannot be comprehensive in a volume of this size it is hoped that the book will encourage newcomers to the subject, and being so handily-sized it is easy to slip into a pocket or backpack while on a walk in the bush. Above all it is hoped that it will inspire and encourage interest in the fascinating study of Australian birds.

THE BIRDS

CASUARIIDAE

SOUTHERN CASSOWARY *Casuarius casuarius*

SIZE/ID: Up to 2m tall. Adult black with blue and red bare skin on head and neck. Female larger than male, with larger casque on head and brighter colours. Immature plain brown; chick boldly striped.

FOOD/BEHAVIOUR: Fungi, small animals, fruit and berries; will eat almost anything. Solitary for most of year, but as breeding season approaches pairs spend time together. Females can mate with up to three males during a breeding season. Males incubate and rear the young.

HABITAT/RANGE: Tropical rainforest in north-east Queensland. Difficult to see as their colours blend with surroundings.

VOICE: A variety of booms, hisses and rumbles.

DROMAIIDAE

EMU *Dromaius novaehollandiae*

SIZE/ID: Up to 2m tall. Flightless and nomadic. Generally brown to grey with bluish skin and blackish down around head. Legs dark brown. Chicks dark brown with cream stripes.

FOOD/BEHAVIOUR: Feeds on plant material. Breeding commences in winter. Female lays up to 20 eggs, male then takes over to hatch and rear young while female searches for another male to lay another clutch of eggs. Young remain with male for 18 months.

HABITAT/RANGE: Widespread and fairly common in a range of habitats from desert areas to timbered country. Absent from densely forest and from Tasmania.

VOICE: Deep grunts or a boom.

ANSERANATIDAE

MAGPIE GOOSE *Anseranas semipalmata*

SIZE/ID: 85cm, male larger. Head, neck, wings, rump and tail black; wing-coverts, mantle and belly white. Legs and partly-webbed feet mainly yellowish. Size of bump on head can indicate age.

FOOD/BEHAVIOUR: Feeds mainly on bulbs of spike rushes, which are dug up on sun-baked mud plains. Breeds usually from February, depending on water-levels and availability of food. Roosts in paperbark trees at night, flying out at dawn.

HABITAT/RANGE: Northern parts of Western Australia and Northern Territory and in north and east Queensland. Prefers swamp areas, usually not more than 100km from the coast.

VOICE: A loud and resonant honking.

ANATIDAE

CAPE BARREN GOOSE *Cereopsis novaehollandiae*

SIZE/ID: Male 90cm, female 80cm. Fairly uniform pale grey with small dark spots on wing-feathers and a whitish crown. Legs pinkish and feet black. Green-yellow cere covers most of bill.

FOOD/BEHAVIOUR: Feeds on grasses and water plants. Often in pairs; thought to mate for life. Very intolerant of other geese.

HABITAT/RANGE: Found along the coast of Victoria, in parts of Tasmania and South Australia and in a small area on the south coast of Western Australia. Endemic to Australia. Early settlers hunted these birds for both eggs and meat but they are now protected.

VOICE: A low-pitched grunt, honk or trumpet.

ANATIDAE

PLUMED WHISTLING-DUCK *Dendrocygna eytoni*

SIZE/ID: Male 60cm, female 50cm. Pale brownish overall. Belly and lower breast chestnut with dark barring. Long yellowish plumes along flanks. Bill speckled pink and blackish.

FOOD/BEHAVIOUR: Legumes form main part of diet; also grass seeds. During dry conditions can gather in flocks of several hundred. Breeds in wet season, when males' courtship activity becomes quite intense.

HABITAT/RANGE: From north Western Australia across Northern Territory, Queensland, New South Wales and into Victoria. Greatest numbers occur in grasslands in Barkly Tablelands, Queensland.

VOICE: A high-pitched monosyllabic whistle; also a twittering flight-call.

ANATIDAE

WANDERING WHISTLING-DUCK
Dendrocygna arcuata

SIZE/ID: Male 60cm, female 55cm. Dark crown and nape contrast with pale face. Dark feathers on back edged with chestnut. Rufous underparts. Yellowish plumes along flanks. Bill plain blackish.

FOOD/BEHAVIOUR: About 99 per cent of diet is aquatic vegetation, including submerged plants, water lilies, grass, duckweed and sedges. Breeding occurs during or after wet season.

HABITAT/RANGE: Favours tropical areas in Western Australia, Northern Territory and into Queensland. Range extends into New South Wales; reports from the Murray River presumably relate to vagrants.

VOICE: A high-pitched shrill whistle, sometimes also a short twitter.

ANATIDAE

BLACK SWAN *Cygnus atratus*

SIZE/ID: 130cm. All black except for red bill and white flight feathers, which are most obvious when the bird is airborne.

FOOD/BEHAVIOUR: At home on land and in water, swans spend as much of the day feeding on grass as they do on aquatic plants. When feeding it is common to see them with tail pointing to the sky and head and neck submerged in the water.

HABITAT/RANGE: Found in wetlands across much of Australia, including Tasmania. Absent from the arid centre. If swans nest on islands or in a rookery, many nests are destroyed as pairs rob each other for material. Up to 10 pale blue-green eggs can be laid and both birds share incubation and cygnet-rearing duties.

VOICE: A variable repertoire of deep, long trumpet calls.

ANATIDAE

AUSTRALIAN SHELDUCK *Tadorna tadornoides*

Male.

Female.

SIZE/ID: Male 70cm, female 60cm. Mainly black with white collar, rufous neck and breast and white, green and rufous on wing. Female has white eye-ring and white base to bill.

FOOD/BEHAVIOUR: Cereal crops, invertebrates and water plants. They appear to pair for life and banding has shown that mating pairs return to the same area each year. Breeding pairs very aggressive towards other shelducks.

HABITAT/RANGE: Mainly in wetlands in Western Australia, South Australia, Victoria, New South Wales and Tasmania. Contrary to the colloquial name of 'mountain duck' these birds do not frequent uplands.

VOICE: A loud honking.

ANATIDAE

RADJAH SHELDUCK *Tadorna radjah*

SIZE/ID: Female 55cm, male 50cm. Head, neck and breast white. Back is a rich chestnut colour and a narrow chestnut band runs across the breast. Bill and legs pink.

FOOD/BEHAVIOUR: Feeds on molluscs, worms, insects and plants including algae and sedges. It is thought these birds pair for life and it is common to see small groups feeding on swampland.

HABITAT/RANGE: Tropical wetlands. Breeds in the top end of Western Australia, Northern Territory and Queensland.

VOICE: Male has a harsh whistle, female a harsh rattling call.

ANATIDAE

AUSTRALIAN WOOD DUCK *Chenonetta jubata*

Male.

Female.

SIZE/ID: 48cm. Grey body with brown head and black rump and tail. Female and immature more heavily spotted underneath and with pale stripes above and below eye. Also known as Maned Duck or Maned Goose due to small crest.

FOOD/BEHAVIOUR: A variety of aquatic plants and grasses. Often seen in pastures. Flocks can commute several kilometres each day between favoured roosting, feeding and breeding areas.

HABITAT/RANGE: Areas with water in Victoria, New South Wales, Queensland and Tasmania, parts of South Australia and Northern Territory, and west of Western Australia.

VOICE: Long mournful call.

ANATIDAE

PACIFIC BLACK DUCK *Anas superciliosa*

SIZE/ID: 61cm. Feathers on body dark brown with pale fringes. Head and neck paler brown with darker crown and eye-stripe and dark line running from base of bill across paler cheek.

FOOD/BEHAVIOUR: Feeds by dabbling on water's surface with a forward movement, and also takes small insects, crustaceans such as yabbies and fairy shrimps and seed from aquatic plants that grow on the water's edge.

HABITAT/RANGE: Probably our most common duck. Found over much of Australia, including Tasmania, in all kinds of wetlands.

VOICE: Loud raucous quack. Male hisses.

ANATIDAE

CHESTNUT TEAL *Anas castanea*

SIZE/ID: 48cm. Male has glossy green head, brown back and chestnut underparts with white patch on rear flank bordering black area around tail. Both sexes have red eye and blue-grey bill. Female has plain dark brown head and dark brown body feathers with pale edges.

FOOD/BEHAVIOUR: Dabbles close to water's edge. Diet varied and feeds in both fresh and salt water. Often roosts on logs or rocks.

HABITAT/RANGE: Inhabits a variety of wetlands in Tasmania, Victoria, New South Wales, south-east South Australia and coastal areas of southern Western Australia and Queensland. Mainly sedentary.

VOICE: Female utters a rapid 'quack', male a muted 'peep'.

ANATIDAE

HARDHEAD *Aythya australis*

SIZE/ID: 49cm. Plain dark chestnut with obvious white undertail-coverts. Grey bill has pale subterminal band. Eye white in male, dark in female. In flight has broad white wing-bars and wings make an audible whir.

FOOD/BEHAVIOUR: Dives for submerged plants, invertebrates and small fish.

HABITAT/RANGE: Relatively sedentary but can become nomadic during drought.

VOICE: Female has a harsh croak, male a soft whistle.

ANATIDAE

BLUE-BILLED DUCK *Oxyura australis*

SIZE/ID: 44cm. Stiff tail often held upright. Male has blue bill, black head and chestnut body, female fairly uniform grey-brown with grey bill.

FOOD/BEHAVIOUR: Dives under surface to feed on plant and animal food.

HABITAT/RANGE: Widespread in Victoria, New South Wales and Tasmania, also found in eastern South Australia and southern Western Australia.

VOICE: Usually silent although male can utter a soft rattle.

ANATIDAE

MUSK DUCK *Biziura lobata*

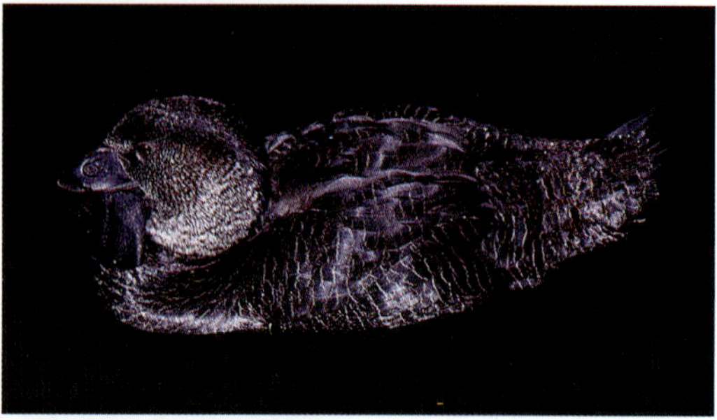

Male.

Female.

SIZE/ID: Male 70cm, female 50cm. Plumage uniform blackish with fine white barring. Male has lobe under bill and musky odour.

FOOD/BEHAVIOUR: Diet mostly animal-based with some plants. Displaying male kicks out a jet of water, often to a distance of 2m, and expands a bladder under the bill to a diameter of about 15cm. Tail feathers raised and spread like a fan over body.

HABITAT/RANGE: Swamps throughout Victoria, New South Wales and Tasmania, also in parts of Western Australia, South Australia and Queensland.

VOICE: Displaying male utters piercing whistle with each kick of leg.

MEGAPODIIDAE

MALLEEFOWL *Leipoa ocellata*

SIZE/ID: 60cm. Head and neck grey with brown throat and black and white streaking in a line down centre of breast. Upperparts heavily spotted and barred brown, including bold rufous heart-shaped markings.

FOOD/BEHAVIOUR: A variety of seed, including acacia, herbs and some insects. Male digs hole for nest, up to 1m deep and 3–4m in diameter, then sweeps forest material into hole and forms mound. Male controls incubation temperature by using bill as a thermometer – when too hot he opens the mound, when too cold more material is added.

HABITAT/RANGE: Occurs locally in dry timbered areas of Western and South Australia, Victoria and New South Wales.

VOICE: Loud booming grunt, when birds are together a soft 'cluck cluck'.

MEGAPODIIDAE

AUSTRALIAN BRUSH-TURKEY *Alectura lathami*

SIZE/ID: 70cm. Bare red skin on head and neck bordered by yellow wattles on sides of neck. Plumage mainly black with fine white scaling on belly. Strong legs and fan-shaped tail. Also known as 'scrub-turkey'.

FOOD/BEHAVIOUR: Feeds mainly on insects, fruit and seeds. Manner of nest-building similar to that of Malleefowl. Male prepares nest so that material soon ferments, and male then works constantly on mound. Mounds which have been used for a number of years can be up to 1.5m high and 4m in diameter.

HABITAT/RANGE: Eastern areas of Queensland and New South Wales. Natural habitat is rainforest. Land clearance has affected range, although they are found in suburbs.

VOICE: A variety of grunts.

PODICIPEDIDAE

AUSTRALASIAN GREBE
Tachybaptus novaehollandiae

SIZE/ID: 25cm. Very small with yellow eye and yellow gape, dark crown and grey-brown body. In breeding season develops black throat and rufous patch on cheek; non-breeding birds have whitish cheek and neck.

FOOD/BEHAVIOUR: Mainly fish. Stomach designed to hold fish bones until they are digested. Very often these birds nest in small colonies and use water plants for building.

HABITAT/RANGE: Found in freshwater wetlands across much of Australia, including in Tasmania. Often seen on water bodies in and around cities.

VOICE: A shrill twitter; the most vocal of all the grebes.

PODICIPEDIDAE

GREAT CRESTED GREBE *Podiceps cristatus*

SIZE/ID: 50cm. Double crest and chestnut frills on the head when breeding. Face and neck white when not breeding. Bill long and pink, back dark grey. Like all grebes can swim a considerable distance under water. White wing-patches obvious in flight.

FOOD/BEHAVIOUR: Fish and aquatic insects and crustaceans. Young often ride on back of parent. Courtship display very elaborate.

HABITAT/RANGE: Widespread in Queensland, New South Wales, Victoria and Tasmania. Localised in Western Australia and South Australia.

VOICE: Threat call 'row-ah, row-ah'.

SPHENISCIDAE

LITTLE PENGUIN *Eudyptula minor*

SIZE/ID: 33cm. Smallest of the world's penguins. Grey-blue above, underparts white, eye whitish, feet flesh-coloured. Also known as 'Fairy Penguin', 'Blue Penguin' and 'Little Blue Penguin'.

FOOD/BEHAVIOUR: Small fish and cephalopods. Nests in a 1m-long burrow. Male and female share nest-building and chick-feeding duties. Chicks usually leave nest at eight weeks.

HABITAT/RANGE: Found from central New South Wales all along the southern coastline of Australia, including Tasmania.

VOICE: Sharp yapping on water, on land a loud braying.

DIOMEDEIDAE

EASTERN YELLOW-NOSED ALBATROSS
Thalassarche carteri

SIZE/ID: 81cm, wingspan 210cm. Head and underparts white, back and upper-tail glossy blackish. Underwing white with narrow black border. Bill mainly black with narrow yellow stripe along top of upper mandible in adult.

FOOD/BEHAVIOUR: Fish and marine invertebrates. Commonly follows fishing boats to feed on fish or offal.

HABITAT/RANGE: Coastal regions south of the Tropic of Capricorn.

VOICE: Loud coughing when fighting for food, also bill-clapping.

DIOMEDEIDAE

SHY ALBATROSS *Thalassarche cauta*

SIZE/ID: 98cm, wingspan 225cm. Back and upperwings slaty grey. Body and head usually white with a dark line running through eye almost to yellowish bill.

FOOD/BEHAVIOUR: Feeds on crustaceans, squid, cuttlefish and carrion. Often follows fishing boats for waste.

HABITAT/RANGE: Common in temperate Australian waters.

VOICE: Bill clapping and a harsh gurgling, gutteral call when feeding or fighting other birds for food.

PROCELLARIIDAE

SHORT-TAILED SHEARWATER *Ardenna tenuirostris*

SIZE/ID: 40cm. Uniform brown-black, except for pale patches on underwings which are visible in flight. Has typical scything 'shearwater' flight and short rounded tail. Also known as 'muttonbird'.

FOOD/BEHAVIOUR: Feeds on krill, cephalopods and fish.

HABITAT/RANGE: Southern coasts from about Perth to Brisbane. Breeds from September in coastal vegetation, often in colonies. Nest often under a tussock. Otherwise pelagic.

VOICE: Noisy repeated 'kooka-rooka-rah'.

HYDROBATIDAE

WHITE-FACED STORM-PETREL
Pelagodroma marina

SIZE/ID: 20cm. Grey above with whitish rump. Underparts and head white with dark grey crown and ear-coverts. Eye, bill and legs dark.

FOOD/BEHAVIOUR: Pelagic. Feeds mainly on plankton. Nest-burrow dug in sand and one white egg laid. Adults gather offshore at dusk and visit the nest in darkness to avoid predators.

HABITAT/RANGE: Southern coasts from about Perth to Brisbane.

VOICE: A loud 'peeoo-peeoo-peeoo'.

SULIDAE

AUSTRALIAN GANNET *Morus serrator*

SIZE/ID: 90cm. Adult white with yellow on head and black face, flight feathers and central tail-feathers. Juvenile dark overall and heavily spotted white.

FOOD/BEHAVIOUR: Fish caught by plunge-diving at great speed into the ocean.

HABITAT/RANGE: Temperate coasts. Nests about 1m apart, often creating tension among the birds.

VOICE: A repetitive 'urrah, urrah'.

PHALACROCORACIDAE

PIED CORMORANT *Phalacrocorax varius*

SIZE/ID: 76cm. White underparts, black upperparts extending to crown. Conspicuous orange-yellow face patch contrasts with long grey bill.

FOOD/BEHAVIOUR: Feeds mainly on small fish, but will eat crustaceans and other marine creatures. Male and female share nest and rearing duties. Cormorants fly in formation.

HABITAT/RANGE: Found all around coastline but rarely inland, venturing at most a few hundred kilometres from coast. Prefers areas where dams, swamps and water holes exist.

VOICE: Cooing, also 'uk-uk-uk'.

ANHINGIDAE

AUSTRALIAN DARTER *Anhinga novaehollandiae*

SIZE/ID: 90cm. Male almost entirely black, with breast brown-black and white streaks on upperparts. Female has white underparts and grey-brown head and neck. Both sexes have white stripe below eye and long, dagger-shaped yellow bill.

FOOD/BEHAVIOUR: Feed mainly on fish, which are speared with the sharp bill. Also takes reptiles, insects and plant life. Highly proficient swimmer, often seen with just head and some neck out of water, at times resembling a snake. During courtship, male builds a small platform in trees above water. Often seen drying outstretched wings.

HABITAT/RANGE: Frequents dams, water holes, swamps and other wetlands. Found over most of Australia, except Tasmania.

VOICE: Breeding calls include 'khaah' and 'tjeeu, krr, kururah'.

PELECANIDAE

AUSTRALIAN PELICAN *Pelecanus conspicillatus*

SIZE/ID: 180cm including 45cm bill, wingspan 250cm. Mainly white with black wings and tail. Eye-ring, bill and pouch pale pink.

FOOD/BEHAVIOUR: Mainly fish. If food supply dwindles during breeding season it is not uncommon for chicks to die from starvation.

HABITAT/RANGE: Found all over Australia, including Tasmania, wherever water is present. They seem to predict where enough rain is falling to produce conditions suitable for breeding. Breeds in colonies.

VOICE: When breeding gives a 'thuh-thuh-thuh' and a gutteral 'oorrh'.

ARDEIDAE

WHITE-NECKED HERON *Ardea pacifica*

SIZE/ID: 91cm. Upperparts grey-black. Head and neck white with double row of black spots down centre of breast. Non-breeding birds lack nuptial plumes, instead having pale chestnut on crown and neck. Also known as 'Pacific Heron'.

FOOD/BEHAVIOUR: Finds fish and other aquatic creatures while wading through water. Breeds whenever there is sufficient food supply. Flies in typical heron fashion with neck folded and head held close to body.

HABITAT/RANGE: Widespread, found in most of Australia.

VOICE: A load croak.

ARDEIDAE

WHITE-FACED HERON *Egretta novaehollandiae*

SIZE/ID: 67cm. Uniform blue-grey, but when airborne flight feathers darker than rest of plumage. Face and throat white, bill dark grey, legs yellow.

FOOD/BEHAVIOUR: Feeds on fish and other small animals. Breeds whenever conditions are suitable. Nest is a platform of sticks, usually in a tall tree.

HABITAT/RANGE: Often seen near water bodies such as lakes, streams and mangrove swamps. Found over all of Australia.

VOICE: A loud croak. At nest gives a gutteral call.

ARDEIDAE

PIED HERON *Egretta picata*

SIZE/ID: 48cm. Plumage dark blue-black with white cheeks and neck. Adult has long black crest and long white feathers hanging down from base of neck. Immature has white crown. Bill and legs yellow.

FOOD/BEHAVIOUR: Invertebrates form an important part of diet; often follow cattle as they disperse insects.

HABITAT/RANGE: Tropical areas of Western Australia, Northern Territory and Queensland. Frequents both salt- and fresh-water, swamps, grasslands and sewage ponds, also meat works and garbage tips.

VOICE: Soft cooing call at nest.

ARDEIDAE

GREAT EGRET *Ardea alba*

SIZE/ID: 83cm. Large white heron with long neck which usually appears longer than body. Legs black and bill yellow. When breeding bill can be blackish and has long white plumes on back which extend beyond tail.

FOOD/BEHAVIOUR: Feeds on fish and other aquatic animals. Breeds at any time of year if conditions are right; the nest is a platform of sticks in a tree above water.

HABITAT/RANGE: Occurs Australia-wide.

VOICE: Low-pitched croak.

ARDEIDAE

CATTLE EGRET *Bubulcus ibis*

SIZE/ID: 53cm. Non-breeding birds white; short bill is yellow and legs yellowish or blackish. In breeding plumage has orange-buff head, breast and back; bill and legs reddish.

FOOD/BEHAVIOUR: Feeds on insects such as grasshoppers and some small aquatic life. It is not uncommon to see these birds following cattle around, waiting to pounce on disturbed insects.

HABITAT/RANGE: Found around the coast of Australia, including Tasmania. Does not venture far inland, usually only about 100km.

VOICE: A loud croaking call, usually at the nest.

ARDEIDAE

NANKEEN NIGHT-HERON *Nycticorax caledonicus*

Immature.

Adult.

SIZE/ID: 48cm. Adult chestnut-brown with black cap. Juvenile boldly spotted and streaked brown and buff. Also known as Rufous Night-Heron.

FOOD/BEHAVIOUR: Feeds on insects, crustaceans, fish and amphibians. Breeds whenever conditions are suitable. Nest usually built of sticks in a tree or bush. Sometimes nests in colonies.

HABITAT/RANGE: Found all over Australia, but absent from arid areas and scarce in Tasmania.

VOICE: Loud croak, usually at night.

THRESKIORNITHIDAE

AUSTRALIAN WHITE IBIS *Threskiornis molucca*

SIZE/ID: 70cm. Plumage white. Bare head and neck, long decurved bill, legs and wing-tips all blackish.

FOOD/BEHAVIOUR: Takes prey such as mussels, crustaceans, frogs and snails. Parents feed young by regurgitation. Groups often fly in a V-formation with necks outstretched (like spoonbills but unlike egrets).

HABITAT/RANGE: Occurs in Northern Territory, New South Wales and Victoria, and in parts of Western Australia and South Australia. Often seen by lagoons and waterways. Also occurs in city centres.

VOICE: Call 'urk, koaha-taw-taw'.

THRESKIORNITHIDAE

STRAW-NECKED IBIS *Threskiornis spinicollis*

SIZE/ID: 70cm. Plumage blackish overall with green-bronze metallic sheen. Belly and neck whitish, the latter with long plumes in adult. Bill black and legs greyish or pinkish.

FOOD/BEHAVIOUR: Takes fish, frogs, small snakes and insects such as grasshoppers. Feeds in both wet and dry pasture, also in water.

HABITAT/RANGE: Our most common ibis species, found over much of Australia, except in desert areas. Usually associated with water. Nests in colonies, often alongside other ibis species.

VOICE: A long 'u-u-urh'.

THRESKIORNITHIDAE

ROYAL SPOONBILL *Platalea regia*

SIZE/ID: 75cm. Plumage all white. Long spoon-shaped bill and legs black. Breeding birds have long head plumes and buff on breast.

FOOD/BEHAVIOUR: Feeds on fish and other aquatic life. Wades in water with bill open to catch food.

HABITAT/RANGE: Occurs in Australia wherever water is found; absent only from deserts.

VOICE: A single 'chew' and 'cho-cho'.

YELLOW-BILLED SPOONBILL *Platalea flavipes*

SIZE/ID: 89cm. Plumage white. Eye, bill, legs and feet yellow.

FOOD/BEHAVIOUR: Feeds on fish and aquatic invertebrates by wading slowly through water and moving the head from side to side to filter food.

HABITAT/RANGE: Wetlands Australia-wide.

VOICE: A single 'chhee' call.

CICONIIDAE

BLACK-NECKED STORK *Ephippiorhynchus asiaticus*

SIZE/ID: 140cm. In adult bill, head, neck, wings, lower back and tail are black. Rest of body white. Legs long and red. Immature fairly plain greyish-brown. Also known as 'jabiru'.

FOOD/BEHAVIOUR: Mainly fish, but also eats small snakes, frogs, crabs and rodents. Frequents swamps, water holes, mangroves and pools.

HABITAT/RANGE: Tropical areas of Western Australia and Northern Territory, most of Queensland and eastern New South Wales.

VOICE: Usually silent, but grunts and clatters bill at nest.

ACCIPITRIDAE

AUSTRALIAN KITE *Elanus axillaris*

SIZE/ID: 36cm. Upperparts pale grey, wings a little darker with black patch on shoulder. Underparts mostly white except for patch of black on primaries which is visible only in flight.

FOOD/BEHAVIOUR: Diet includes small animals and insects. Usually seen in pairs hovering over open country or perched on poles, diving down when potential prey is spotted.

HABITAT/RANGE: All of Austalia, except arid regions and Tasmania. Prefers woodland areas for nesting and hunting.

VOICE: Common calls include rapid sharp whistles and wheezing.

ACCIPITRIDAE

WEDGE-TAILED EAGLE *Aquila audax*

SIZE/ID: 100cm. Australia's largest bird of prey. Plumage blackish-brown in general. Long wedge-shaped tail is diagnostic, especially in flight.

FOOD/BEHAVIOUR: Takes animals such as rabbits; also snakes, lizards and carrion.

HABITAT/RANGE: Found all over Australia, including Tasmania. Prefers forest land but will frequent open plains when searching for food.

VOICE: Repeated whistle 'yessir', also a loud screech.

FALCONIDAE

AUSTRALIAN HOBBY *Falco longipennis*

Adult.

Immature.

SIZE/ID: 35cm. Slate grey above. Underparts buff with black streaks. Black head bordered by white throat and half-collar. Legs yellow. Also known as 'Little Falcon'.

FOOD/BEHAVIOUR: Takes grasshoppers, dragonflies and winged ants; also small birds, which are caught in flight.

HABITAT/RANGE: Found Australia-wide, including in parts of Tasmania. A very wary bird that frequents open bush and woodlands. Also occurs in cities when there is suitable habitat.

VOICE: A shrill twittering call, repeated a few times.

FALCONIDAE

NANKEEN KESTREL *Falco cenchroides*

Female.

Male.

SIZE/ID: 35cm. Upperparts rufous with dark spotting. Has dark moustache, flight feathers and subterminal tail-band. Underparts whitish with fine streaks.

FOOD/BEHAVIOUR: Feeds on prey such as rodents and insects. Often hovers while hunting.

HABITAT/RANGE: Prefers open country for feeding. Also occurs in cities, particularly near wasteland or garbage tips. Found Australia-wide.

VOICE: A shrill 'ki ki ki'.

OTIDIDAE

AUSTRALIAN BUSTARD *Ardeotis australis*

SIZE/ID: 120cm, wingspan 230cm. Upperparts brown, underparts white, neck and head grey with black crown. Legs yellowish.

FOOD/BEHAVIOUR: Diet little known, but takes grasshoppers, crickets and seed from native fruits, and probably also mice and small reptiles. When displaying male inflates neck-pouch and extends neck-feathers.

HABITAT/RANGE: Only found in dry parts of Australia. Favoured areas include open country of Barkly Tablelands and Kimberleys.

VOICE: Usually silent, but has low booming call when breeding.

TURNICIDAE

PAINTED BUTTONQUAIL *Turnix varius*

SIZE/ID: Resembles a quail but unrelated. Mottled brown and blue-grey overall with rufous on sides of breast. Heavily marked all over with black and white spots and streaks.

FOOD/BEHAVIOUR: Plant matter such as grass seeds and fruits.

HABITAT/RANGE: Eastern Australia from central Queensland to central South Australia. Also Tasmania and south-west Western Australia.

VOICE: Repeated 'pink pink pink'.

RALLIDAE

BUFF-BANDED RAIL *Gallirallus philippensis*

SIZE/ID: 31cm. Face and nape rufous, supercilium white, crown brown. Upperparts streaked brownish. Underparts finely barred black and white with orange-buff band across breast. Bill long and red.

FOOD/BEHAVIOUR: Small invertebrates and seeds. Rarely flies when disturbed, instead runs away quickly. Has a habit of flicking tail when frightened.

HABITAT/RANGE: Common around swamps, lagoons and water holes, although not often seen. Occurs widely in eastern Australia from Queensland to Victoria, also in south-west Western Australia.

VOICE: A creaky 'swit swit'.

RALLIDAE

PURPLE SWAMPHEN *Porphyrio porphyria*

SIZE/ID: 48cm. Rich blue-purple all over, brightest on breast. Bill and frontal shield bright red. Legs can be red, pink or brown. Also known as 'Eastern Swamphen'.

FOOD/BEHAVIOUR: Possibly the main diet is tender reed stems. Also eats seeds and animals including frogs and molluscs.

HABITAT/RANGE: Found over much of Australia including Tasmania, but rare in the arid regions. Often seen in water, but equally at home on land.

VOICE: Call is a loud, screeching 'kee-oww'.

RALLIDAE

DUSKY MOORHEN *Gallinula tenebrosa*

SIZE/ID: 35cm. Slaty-black with washed-brown above and white patches on each side of undertail. Red bill and legs, the former with yellow tip.

FOOD/BEHAVIOUR: Feeds in water and on land, mainly on plants and insects.

HABITAT/RANGE: Widespread in eastern Australia, also occurs in south-west Western Australia. Prefers swamps to open water.

VOICE: Usually silent, apart from a clear 'kurk'.

EURASIAN COOT *Fulica atra*

SIZE/ID: 39cm. Uniform greyish-black with red eye and white frontal shield and bill. Legs grey with large lobes on toes.

FOOD/BEHAVIOUR: Food mainly plants. Common in parks where people feed them.

HABITAT/RANGE: Australia-wide. Common wherever fresh water is abundant.

VOICE: A single 'kowk' is the most common call.

GRUIDAE

BROLGA *Grus rubicunda*

SIZE/ID: 125cm. Very long neck and legs. Plumage grey. Bill green-grey or yellowish. Has bare red skin around throat, face and nape.

FOOD/BEHAVIOUR: Main diet is sedge tubers, insects and other water creatures. The dance of Brolgas is something special and people who have witnessed this spectacle are truly blessed.

HABITAT/RANGE: Range extends from north Western Australia east to Queensland and then south to Victoria and a small area of South Australia. Feeds on crops and swamp areas.

VOICE: A loud trumpeting call 'kawee-kreee-kurr-kurr-kurr'.

BURHINIDAE

BUSH STONE-CURLEW *Burhinus grallarius*

SIZE/ID: 55cm. Plumage mainly brown and heavily streaked. Has broad pale panel in wing and a black band runs from eye and down side of neck. Underparts pale buff with fine dark streaking. Long yellowish legs and large yellow eye.

FOOD/BEHAVIOUR: Nocturnal, feeds mainly on invertebrates. Nest is a scrape on the ground, usually near a dead tree or limb. With their cryptic markings these birds excel in camouflage.

HABITAT/RANGE: Patchily distributed over much of Australia in bushland with clearings.

VOICE: Mournful and high-pitched wailing 'wee-loo' or 'wer-loo'.

RECURVIROSTRIDAE

WHITE-HEADED STILT *Himantopus leucocephalus*

SIZE/ID: 38.5cm. Long pink legs and fine black bill. Back of head, nape and wings black. Head, neck and underparts white. Also known as 'Pied Stilt' and 'Black-winged Stilt'.

FOOD/BEHAVIOUR: Wades in shallows to feed on aquatic plants and animals. Nomadic, wandering in search of suitable habitat.

HABITAT/RANGE: Found in wetlands, swamps, lakes and estuaries Australia-wide; rare in arid regions.

VOICE: A dog-like yelp.

RECURVIROSTRIDAE

AUSTRALIAN PIED OYSTERCATCHER
Haematopus longirostris

SIZE/ID: 48cm. Upperparts, head and breast black. Has white rump, belly, flanks and narrow wing-bar. Eye scarlet with orange eye-ring. Bill bright orange, legs pink.

FOOD/BEHAVIOUR: Feeds on marine molluscs, mainly in estuaries when the tide has retreated. It is not uncommon to see oystercatchers with their bill buried in sand in search of hidden prey.

HABITAT/RANGE: Frequents beaches and estuaries around Australia's coastline. Tasmania and the Bass Strait islands are an important wintering area and flocks of several hundred birds are not uncommon.

VOICE: Clear and penetrating 'he-eep'.

CHARADRIIDAE

MASKED LAPWING *Vanellus miles*

SIZE/ID: 33cm. Olive-brown back and white underparts, neck and head with black crown. Has yellow eye, bill and bare skin on face which forms a wattle below each eye. In flight has broad, rounded wings with bold black-and-pale pattern.

FOOD/BEHAVIOUR: Invertebrates form bulk of diet. Very agressive during breeding season. When not breeding can form nomadic flocks of several hundred birds.

HABITAT/RANGE: Found over much of Australia. They frequent wetlands and are often seen in farm pasture, as well in towns, on nature strips and in gardens.

VOICE: Loud 'keer-kick-ki-ki-ki'.

CHARADRIIDAE

BANDED LAPWING *Vanellus tricolor*

SIZE/ID: 25cm. Brown upperparts and white throat, belly and stripe behind eye. Has black crown, breast-band and sides of neck. Bill and eye yellow. Has small red wattles above bill.

FOOD/BEHAVIOUR: Feeds mainly on seeds, grasses, herbage, insects and small vertebrates. Flaps wings very slowly in flight. Congregates more for feeding than Masked Lapwing.

HABITAT/RANGE: Resident in many parts of Australia except the far north. Nomadic and appears to prefer dry unimproved country, often near water.

VOICE: Call 'chee-chee-chee'.

CHARADRIIDAE

RED-CAPPED PLOVER *Charadrius ruficapillus*

SIZE/ID: 15cm. Sandy-brown upperparts and white underparts and forehead. Breeding male has rufous crown and nape and black eyestripe and border to crown. Female lacks black and has paler rufous on crown.

FOOD/BEHAVIOUR: Takes various invertebrates, including insects, worms and molluscs, and possibly also seeds from aquatic plants.

HABITAT/RANGE: Found all around the Australian coastline, often on sand- and mudflats. Also in tidal inlets and inland where permanent water is located.

VOICE: Main call 'twink-twink'.

CHARADRIIDAE

BLACK-FRONTED DOTTEREL *Elseyornis melanops*

SIZE/ID: 16cm. Largely sandy-brown above and white below with black forehead, mask and breast-band. Rump and shoulder-patch rufous. Bill orange with black tip.

FOOD/BEHAVIOUR: Feeds on a variety of insects and small aquatic animals. Often feeds around tidal areas. It is not uncommon for a pair to live permanently on a dam or water hole.

HABITAT/RANGE: Found all over Australia including Tasmania, except for a small area of central and western Australia. A familar bird in swamps and freshwater wetlands. Favourite habitat is stony river-beds.

VOICE: Usual call 'chip-chip-chip-chip'.

CHARADRIIDAE

HOODED PLOVER *Thinornis rubricollis*

SIZE/ID: 20cm. Pale brown above and white below. Head and throat black with broad white nape and black border on upper back. Legs pale orange, bill and eye-ring bright orange.

FOOD/BEHAVIOUR: Feeds on a variety of marine creatures including insects and small fish.

HABITAT/RANGE: Sandy areas and mudflats along southern coasts of Australia, including Tasmania, from Perth to Sydney.

VOICE: Mainly silent, although has a deep barking 'fow-fow-fow'.

LARIDAE

SILVER GULL *Chroicocephalus novaehollandiae*

SIZE/ID: 42.5cm. Plumage predominantly white with grey upperparts and black wing-tips. Bill, legs and eye-ring bright red in adult and brownish in juvenile, while the latter also has dark eye.

FOOD/BEHAVIOUR: Feeds on a variety of marine creatures such as crustaceans. Also follows fishing boats for scraps, feeds on waste on garbage tips, frequents recently ploughed paddocks in search of worms, and feeds on eggs of ground-nesting birds.

HABITAT/RANGE: A common bird all around the coast of Australia. Also occurs inland in some areas, nesting on lakes.

VOICE: A harsh 'kwarr'.

LARIDAE

PACIFIC GULL *Larus pacificus*

SIZE/ID: 63.5cm. Huge black-backed gull with white head and underparts. In flight shows white trailing edge to wing and black band on tail. Red-tipped yellow bill looks disproportionately large. Juvenile mottled grey-brown.

FOOD/BEHAVIOUR: Usually solitary. Feeds on squid, crabs and molluscs; will crack open turbo shells by dropping them from air. Also feeds on young birds.

HABITAT/RANGE: Coasts of New South Wales, Victoria, Tasmania, South Australia and south Western Australia.

VOICE: A deep 'kiaw kiaw'.

LARIDAE

CASPIAN TERN *Hydroprogne caspia*

SIZE/ID: 56cm. Massive orange-red bill. Crown, forehead and nape black when breeding. Non-breeding birds have black mask and speckled crown. Underparts white, upperparts grey. Tail has shallow fork.

FOOD/BEHAVIOUR: Plunge-dives to catch fish. Nests in colonies on sand.

HABITAT/RANGE: All around Australian coast.

VOICE: Loud and deep 'kraah, kraah'.

GREATER CRESTED TERN *Thalasseus bergii*

SIZE/ID: 46cm. Pale yellow bill, white underparts and grey back, white forehead and black erectile crest. Crown black when breeding, speckled otherwise.

FOOD/BEHAVIOUR: Dives into water to feed on fish. Hunting birds indicate presence of schools of fish to fishermen.

HABITAT/RANGE: All around the coast of Australia.

VOICE: Alarm note 'wep-wep-wep'.

LARIDAE

FAIRY TERN *Sternula nereis*

SIZE/ID: 25cm, wingspan 50cm. Small tern. Pale grey above and white below with black rear-crown and white forehead. Bill and legs yellow when breeding, blackish in non-breeding plumage. Tail white and forked.

FOOD/BEHAVIOUR: Feeds on small fish and other aquatic life by plunge-diving.

HABITAT/RANGE: Southern coastal areas from Western Australia to Victoria and Tasmania. Very common in the west and in winter vast flocks have been seen migrating.

VOICE: High-pitched 'krik-krik-krik'.

LARIDAE

WHISKERED TERN *Chlidonias hybrida*

SIZE/ID: 26cm. Small tern. Pale grey above. When breeding has black crown, white cheek, grey breast and belly and dark red bill and legs. Non-breeding birds resemble Fairy Tern with all-black bill and legs, but have greyish tail with shallow fork.

FOOD/BEHAVIOUR: Feeds mainly on insects which are caught on the wing or picked off the water's surface. Rarely plunge-dives.

HABITAT/RANGE: Found over much of Australia, but absent from Tasmania. Breeds by fresh water, also found on coasts.

VOICE: High-pitched 'kreek-kreek' and 'kek-kek-kek-kek'.

COLUMBIDAE

WHITE-HEADED PIGEON *Columba leucomela*

SIZE/ID: 40cm. Male has creamy-white head and upperparts black with purple sheen. Female similar but paler shades.

FOOD/BEHAVIOUR: Feeds on native and cultivated fruits and maize and stubble.

HABITAT/RANGE: Rainforest and cultivated areas from coastal Queensland to south-east Victoria.

VOICE: Deep 'cook-cook'.

EMERALD DOVE *Chalcophaps indica*

SIZE/ID: 25cm. Upperparts emerald green with white on shoulder. Head, underparts and tail rufous-brown. Male slightly more colourful than female.

FOOD/BEHAVIOUR: Feeds on a variety of seeds and fruit; often eats fallen figs.

HABITAT/RANGE: Coastal areas from north Western Australia through Northern Territory and Queensland and into New South Wales.

VOICE: Penetrating and repeated 'coo, coo, coo'.

COLUMBIDAE

COMMON BRONZEWING *Phaps chalcoptera*

SIZE/ID: 35cm. Has scaly brown back, iridescent bronze and green spots on wings bordered by white, and white line running below eye. Male has cream forehead and purple-brown breast, female has grey forehead and buff-brown breast.

FOOD/BEHAVIOUR: Grain makes up about 50 per cent of the diet, the balance is from patterson's curse, pasture seed, acacia and kurrajong trees. Drinks at dawn and dusk.

HABITAT/RANGE: Found over most of Australia, including Tasmania.

VOICE: Soft, deep 'oom oom'.

COLUMBIDAE

CRESTED PIGEON *Ocyphaps lophotes*

SIZE/ID: 35cm. Pale grey underparts and head with long, slender, upright crest. Upperparts grey-brown and barred. Iridescent bronze and green feathers on wing. Red legs and eye-ring.

FOOD/BEHAVIOUR: Varied diet includes grain, green leaves, insects, barley grass, thistles and other plant seeds.

HABITAT/RANGE: Found over much of the Australian mainland. Absent from Tasmania.

VOICE: Call a low wavering 'coo, coo'.

COLUMBIDAE

SPINIFEX PIGEON *Geophaps plumifera*

SIZE/ID: 22.5cm. Mostly rufous-brown with barred upperparts and long upright crest. White throat bordered by black band. Red patch surrounds eye.

FOOD/BEHAVIOUR: Mainly seeds and plants. Well adapted to desert life and rarely needs to drink.

HABITAT/RANGE: Dry areas of spinifex from central Australia north and west to coasts of Northern Territory and Western Australia.

VOICE: A soft low-pitched 'oom'.

WONGA PIGEON *Leucosarcia picata*

SIZE/ID: 38cm. Upperparts and breast slate-grey. Has white forehead and two white lines through dark breast. Belly and flanks white with dark spots.

FOOD/BEHAVIOUR: Feeds on ground on fruit and seeds. Solitary outside breeding season.

HABITAT/RANGE: Occurs close to coast from south-east Queensland to Victoria; rarely ventures more than a few hundred kilometres inland.

VOICE: High-pitched 'coo-coo-coo'.

COLUMBIDAE

DIAMOND DOVE *Geopelia cuneata*

SIZE/ID: 20cm. Head, neck and breast pale blue-grey. Back, rump and upper side of tail grey-brown. White 'diamond' spots on wings, replaced by pale barring in juvenile.

FOOD/BEHAVIOUR: Feeds almost entirely on seeds from a variety of drought plants, herbs and grass. Sometimes feeds on insects.

HABITAT/RANGE: Found over most of Australia except for far south and east coast. Prefers drier areas.

VOICE: Distinct call a mournful 'cooo-oo-oo'.

COLUMBIDAE

PIED IMPERIAL-PIGEON *Ducula bicolor*

SIZE/ID: 44cm. Plumage white, except for black tail and flight feathers. Also known as Torres Strait Pigeon and Torresian Imperial Pigeon.

FOOD/BEHAVIOUR: Diet varies according to the fruiting seasons of different trees, although it is thought that 40 per cent of food comes from fig trees.

HABITAT/RANGE: Mainly a coastal bird that occurs from top area of Western Australia to coastal Queensland. Often breeds on offshore islands.

VOICE: Low-pitched and loud 'ooo-ooo'.

CUCULIDAE

CHANNEL-BILLED CUCKOO
Scythrops novaehollandiae

SIZE/ID: 65cm. Huge with long yellow bill, long tail and long pointed wings. Pale grey with barred belly, dark spots on wings and dark subterminal band on tail. Eye and lores red.

FOOD/BEHAVIOUR: Feeds on fruit such as figs and a variety of insects and small animals. Nest-parasite of birds such as crows and magpies.

HABITAT/RANGE: Coastal areas of New South Wales, Queensland, Northern Territory and northern Western Australia.

VOICE: Raucous 'cark-cark-cark'.

TYTONIDAE

EASTERN BARN OWL *Tyto delicatula*

SIZE/ID: 35cm. Upperparts a mixture of buff and grey, finely spotted on head and mantle and with dark barring on wings. Underparts white. Facial disc white with dark marks in front of eyes.

FOOD/BEHAVIOUR: Nocturnal. Feeds on mice, rats, marsupials and small birds. Population increases in response to plagues of rodents. Spends much of day roosting on tree limb or inside old barn.

HABITAT/RANGE: Found Australia-wide, including Tasmania. Favours open woodland.

VOICE: A long drawn-out screech.

STRIGIDAE

SOUTHERN BOOBOOK *Ninox novaeseelandiae*

SIZE/ID: 32cm. Dark grey-brown above with white spotting. Underparts white with heavy brown spots and streaks. Eyes yellow and has pale border to facial disk.

FOOD/BEHAVIOUR: Feeds on small mammals such as rodents, also birds and insects.

HABITAT/RANGE: Found in woodland areas over much of Australia, including Tasmania.

VOICE: Repetitive 'book-book' call.

PODARGIDAE

TAWNY FROGMOUTH *Podargus strigoides*

SIZE/ID: 46cm. Cryptic plumage. Superficially owl-like but with huge wide bill. Soft grey mottled with brown on shoulders and wing coverts. Tail is grey, as are the underparts.

FOOD/BEHAVIOUR: Eats small animals such as rodents, birds and insects. Unfortunately frogmouths are frequently killed by cars as they fly at night. Sits camouflaged on a branch by day.

HABITAT/RANGE: Forests, parks and gardens Australia-wide.

VOICE: A soft 'ooo ooo', usually only at night.

APODIDAE

WHITE-THROATED NEEDLETAIL
Hirundapus caudacutus

SIZE/ID: 20cm, wingspan 50cm. Mostly blackish with glossy green-black wings, paler brownish back and white forehead, throat and undertail-coverts. Each tail feather has 4mm-long spines.

FOOD/BEHAVIOUR: Insects are the main diet; they feed and drink while flying, and prey is gathered from a few centimetres off the ground to heights of over 100m. They are known to fly through trees to disturb insect prey.

HABITAT/RANGE: Eastern coast of Australia and Tasmania, South Australia, Victoria, New South Wales and Queensland. Often seen ahead of stormy weather.

VOICE: Shrill chattering or twittering.

ALCEDINIDAE

LAUGHING KOOKABURRA *Dacelo novaeguineae*

SIZE/ID: 46cm. The two kookaburra species are the largest members of the kingfisher family. Head off-white with dark mask through eye. Wings dark brown with pale blue markings, tail barred brown and black. Underparts whitish and faintly barred brown.

FOOD/BEHAVIOUR: Takes a wide variety of prey. Snakes, lizards, rodents and small birds are the main items, but also eats insects and other agricultural pests.

HABITAT/RANGE: Woodlands and parks in much of eastern Australia, including Tasmania, and a small area of Western Australia.

VOICE: A rollicking, laughing 'koo-hoo-hoo-hoo-haa-haa-haa'.

ALCEDINIDAE

BLUE-WINGED KOOKABURRA *Dacelo leachii*

SIZE/ID: 46cm. Head and underparts whitish. Crown has fine dark streaks and lacks dark mask of Laughing. Back chocolate-brown. Wing dark blue on flight feathers, sky blue on coverts. Rump sky blue, tail dark blue in male, barred brown and black in female.

FOOD/BEHAVIOUR: Insects, small rodents, birds and other animals.

HABITAT/RANGE: Northern regions of Western Australia, Northern Territory and Queensland. Prefers wet habitats, often seen along creek banks and in wet woodland areas.

VOICE: Starts with a 'huff-huff' and develops into 'ow-ow-ow' and a series of trills.

ALCEDINIDAE

RED-BACKED KINGFISHER
Todiramphhus pyrrhopygius

SIZE/ID: 24cm. Male has blue-green crown and ear-covert and white collar and underparts. Rump and uppertail-coverts are rufous, tail turquoise, wings paler turquoise. Female similar but crown, mantle, tail and wings are duller.

FOOD/BEHAVIOUR: Insects such as grasshoppers, and small animals including frogs, lizards and birds.

HABITAT/RANGE: Found over most of Australia, except Tasmania. A nomadic species which is often seen away from water.

VOICE: Utters a mournful whistle.

ALCEDINIDAE

SACRED KINGFISHER *Todiramphus sanctus*

SIZE/ID: 23cm. Head is dusky turquoise-green, with an ochre-buff spot in front of eye. Mantle and shoulders dusky-green grading to bright turquoise-blue on back. Female similar to male but paler.

FOOD/BEHAVIOUR: Small lizards and insects such as crickets, grasshoppers, beetles and their larvae.

HABITAT/RANGE: Found over much of Australia and parts of Tasmania, plus many of the surrounding islands. Rarely seen in inland regions.

VOICE: Usually utters 'ek-ek-ek-ek'.

MEROPIDAE

RAINBOW BEE-EATER *Merops ornatus*

SIZE/ID: 23cm including long decurved bill and two central tail-feathers which project 2cm. Mainly bright green with black mask through eye. Forehead pale green, crown rufous, rump blue-green and tail blue.

FOOD/BEHAVIOUR: Feeds on insects such as bees, wasps and dragonflies. Sits on limb or log waiting for prey to fly past, then sallies out and catches it on the wing.

HABITAT/RANGE: Found over much of Australia, except Tasmania, in a variety of woodlands. Nests in a burrow, usually in a creek bed, roadside cutting, sandpit or quarry.

VOICE: Constant high-pitched chattering 'chitter-chitter'.

CACATUIDAE

RED-TAILED BLACK COCKATOO
Calyptorhynchus banksii

SIZE/ID: 61cm. Male plain black with red sides to tail. Female black with yellow speckles on head, neck and shoulders, underparts barred yellow and red and yellow barring on sides of tail.

FOOD/BEHAVIOUR: Often seen in trees, feeding on casuarina and some eucalypts. Also hakea, banksia and acacia seeds and cones.

HABITAT/RANGE: Patchily distributed in woodlands in all mainland states. Absent from Tasmania and much of inland and south-east.

VOICE: Harsh grating 'kree-krurr'.

CACATUIDAE

YELLOW-TAILED BLACK COCKATOO
Calyptorhynchus funereus

SIZE/ID: 69cm. Dark brown to black with scaly appearance due to pale yellowish feather-edges. Has large yellow patches on cheek and sides of tail. Eye-ring pink in male, grey in female.

FOOD/BEHAVIOUR: Feeds on larvae of wood-boring insects that are found in eucalypt trees, and also on banksia, pine and hakea cones.

HABITAT/RANGE: Found in forest within a few hundred kilometres of the coastline in south Queensland, New South Wales, Victoria, Tasmania and south-east South Australia.

VOICE: Whistle-like call 'whee-la'.

CACATUIDAE

CARNABY'S BLACK COCKATOO
Calyptorhynchus latirostris

SIZE/ID: 60cm. Plumage mainly brown-black. Feathers edged with pale buff. Has buff-white patch on cheek and tail has broad whitish edges.

FOOD/BEHAVIOUR: Feeds on seeds, hakea and banksia cones and small fruits. Often seen feeding on ground, foraging for roots and other food.

HABITAT/RANGE: Found only in a small area of south-west Western Australia, where it frequents pine forest and open woodland regions.

VOICE: Whistle-like call 'pee-er'.

CACATUIDAE

GANG-GANG COCKATOO *Callocephalon fimbriatum*

SIZE/ID: 35cm. Male has grey plumage with feathers edged white and a bright red head and crest. Eye dark brown, bill horn-coloured and legs grey. Female similar but with grey head and some rufous barring on breast.

FOOD/BEHAVIOUR: fruit and berries. When disturbed a flock will fly from a bush making lots of noise, then return to the same place and carry on feeding like nothing ever happened.

HABITAT/RANGE: Found only in Victoria, south-east New South Wales and Australian Capital Territory. Prefers mountain country but often visits lowland areas to feed.

VOICE: A rasping screech.

CACATUIDAE

MAJOR MITCHELL'S COCKATOO
Lophocroa leadbeateri

SIZE/ID: 36cm. Whitish head and underparts suffused with salmon-pink, wings mostly white. Long crest scarlet in centre and tipped white.

FOOD/BEHAVIOUR: Nuts, seeds, grain and cypress and pine cones. Spends much of day feeding on ground, otherwise often rests in trees where a frequent habit is to pull leaves off branches.

HABITAT/RANGE: Patchy distribution. Occurs in all states except Tasmania, but mainly found away from coasts in arid inland regions in places with permanent water.

VOICE: Three or four harsh screeches.

CACATUIDAE

GALAH *Eolophus roseicapillus*

SIZE/ID: 36cm. Crown and nape pale pink. Rest of head and underparts bright pink. Wings, tail, bill, legs and feet grey. Eye-ring pink in male, grey in female.

FOOD/BEHAVIOUR: Feeds on any grain and seeds of grasses that are on ground. Usually feeds in flocks, with some birds watching for predators while others feed.

HABITAT/RANGE: Found all over mainland Australia and in some parts of Tasmania.

VOICE: A variety of harsh screeches.

CACATUIDAE

LONG-BILLED CORELLA *Cacatua tenuirostris*

SIZE/ID: 37.5cm. Mainly white with short crest and yellowish underside to wings and tail visible in flight. Pink-red on face and upper breast.

FOOD/BEHAVIOUR: Onion grass, other plants and grain. Often digs in soil and plumage can become dirty.

HABITAT/RANGE: Open woodland from south-east South Australia through Victoria and New South Wales and into Queensland. Feral in south-west Western Australia.

VOICE: A strong shriek when alarmed.

LITTLE CORELLA *Cacatua sanguinea*

SIZE/ID: 38cm. White with grey skin around eye and reddish lores. No crest, but raises crown-feathers when alarmed.

FOOD/BEHAVIOUR: Legumes and grains. Gregarious and often loud when feeding.

HABITAT/RANGE: Prefers dry areas over much of Australia.

VOICE: Shrieks when alarmed; contact call is more of a chuckle.

CACATUIDAE

SULPHUR-CRESTED COCKATOO *Cacatua galerita*

SIZE/ID: 49cm. Plumage all white with yellow crest, which is frequently raised. The naked eye ring is white and the eye dark brown. Bill grey-black and legs dark grey.

FOOD/BEHAVIOUR: Feeds on seed gathered from ground, roots, nuts and buds. During the day will often perch in trees just stripping the bark and leaves.

HABITAT/RANGE: Population has increased in recent years as birds have adapted to a wider variety of habitats, and can often be seen in new areas, including city centres. Absent from arid areas. Found from northern Western Australia across the north and east of the country and as far south as Adelaide and Tasmania. Introduced population around Perth.

VOICE: Raucous contact call given in flight; more raucous when alarmed.

CACATUIDAE

COCKATIEL *Nymphicus hollandicus*

SIZE/ID: 32cm, including tail of 15cm. Plumage mainly grey, underparts a little paler. Forehead, cheeks and throat yellow with orange patch at ear and large white patch on wings.

FOOD/BEHAVIOUR: Seeds, herbaceous plants, grain and berries including mistletoe.

HABITAT/RANGE: Found over most of mainland Australia; absent from Tasmania.

VOICE: A prolonged warble and 'queel-queel' call.

PSITTACULIDAE

SUPERB PARROT *Polytelis swainsonii*

SIZE/ID: 40cm, including 26cm tail. Plumage mainly bright green. Male has rich yellow throat and cheek-patches with scarlet bar across lower throat. Female lacks red and yellow and has paler-looking face with blue-green cheek and throat.

FOOD/BEHAVIOUR: Nectar, fruits, leaf buds and some grains.

HABITAT/RANGE: Only found in open forest in small areas of central New South Wales and Victoria.

VOICE: A long and deep warble, much deeper than other similar species.

PSITTACULIDAE

REGENT PARROT *Polytelis anthopeplus*

SIZE/ID: 40cm, including 20cm tail. Male has olive-yellow head, underparts and shoulder, green back and dark blue wings and tail with red patch on coverts. Female plain olive-green, but still with red patch on wing.

FOOD/BEHAVIOUR: Grain, fruit and buds. Often feeds on ground.

HABITAT/RANGE: Open forest in south-west Western Australia and inland around the borders of South Australia, Victoria and New South Wales.

VOICE: A soft twittering call.

PRINCESS PARROT *Polytelis alexandrae*

SIZE/ID: 45cm, including 28cm tail. Male has blue crown, pink throat, grey underparts, olive upperparts and yellow-green shoulder. Female similar but paler.

FOOD/BEHAVIOUR: Often feeds on ground in search on plants including spinifex and native grasses.

HABITAT/RANGE: Nomadic. Only in arid central regions.

VOICE: When flushed from trees utters a soft twittering call.

PSITTACULIDAE

AUSTRALIAN KING PARROT *Alisterus scapularis*

SIZE/ID: 43cm, including 20cm tail. Male has brilliant scarlet head and underparts, dark green upperparts with pale green stripe on wing and blue collar and tail. Female has orange-red belly and dark green head, breast and upperparts.

FOOD/BEHAVIOUR: Feeds mainly on seed and grain. Sometimes attracted to crops of maize and fruit. Usually seen in pairs or small flocks.

HABITAT/RANGE: Found not far from the coast from northern Queensland through New South Wales to Victoria. Often favours mountain ranges.

VOICE: Flight call is a shrill and frequently repeated 'crassak-crassak'.

Male.

Female.

PSITTACULIDAE

RED-WINGED PARROT *Aprosmictus erythropterus*

Male.

Female.

SIZE/ID: 33cm. Male's plumage mainly bright green with darker back and wings and large red patch on shoulder. Female dull green overall with some yellow-green on rump and belly and smaller red patch on wing.

FOOD/BEHAVIOUR: Grain, fruits including mistletoe, and seeds including eucalypt and acacia.

HABITAT/RANGE: Found from north of Western Australia and Northern Territory through much of Queensland and New South Wales. Prefers lightly timbered country.

VOICE: Calls include a sharp 'crillik-crillik'; alarm call is a shrill screech.

PSITTACULIDAE

ECLECTUS PARROT *Eclectus roratus*

SIZE/ID: 43cm. Male has brilliant green plumage with blue on wings, reddish on sides of breast and orange bill. Female has brilliant red head, dark red back, blue breast and collar and blackish bill.

FOOD/BEHAVIOUR: Feeds on berries, fruits, nuts and tropical blossoms. A swift flier, which when frightened will fly high into the air with loud screeching.

HABITAT/RANGE: Found only in a small area of the Cape York Peninsula in tropical north Queensland.

VOICE: Contact call in flight is 'krraach-krraak', repeated several times.

PSITTACULIDAE

BOURKE'S PARROT *Neopsephotos bourkii*

SIZE/ID: 19cm. Upperparts brownish and heavily scaled due to broad pale edges. Shoulders and flight feathers suffused with blue. Throat and breast brown in female, pink in male.

FOOD/BEHAVIOUR: Seeds and grasses. Nomadic during drought.

HABITAT/RANGE: Dry inland areas in all mainland states except Victoria. Mainly in mulga and open woodlands.

VOICE: Repeated 'chu-wee chu-wee'. Shrill disyllablic alarm.

BLUE-WINGED PARROT *Neophema chrysostoma*

SIZE/ID: 21cm. Green with yellow on belly and around eye, blue on forehead and tail and extensive blue patch on wing.

FOOD/BEHAVIOUR: Seeds of wallaby grass and other plants, blossom, fruit and insects.

HABITAT/RANGE: Widespread in Victoria, New South Wales and Tasmania.

VOICE: A sharp, high-pitched, buzzing two-syllable call.

PSITTACULIDAE

ELEGANT PARROT *Neophema elegans*

SIZE/ID: 22.5cm including 11cm tail. Upperparts and breast rich golden-olive, with yellow on face and belly and blue on forehead, tail and wings.

FOOD/BEHAVIOUR: Feeds on grasses and other plants such as clovers, as well as berries and fruits. Often seen in pairs during breeding season and flocks of up to a few hundred birds otherwise.

HABITAT/RANGE: Open forest, mainly in south-west Western Australia, south-east South Australia and western Victoria.

VOICE: A sharp 'tsit-tsit-tsit'.

PSITTACULIDAE

ORANGE-BELLIED PARROT *Neophema chrysogaster*

SIZE/ID: 20.5cm, including 10.5cm tail. Similar to Elegant Parrot with bright green plumage and blue on forehead, wings and tail. Differs in having a patch of bright orange-red on belly.

FOOD/BEHAVIOUR: Seeds of grasses, shrubs and saltmarsh plants, as well as fruit.

HABITAT/RANGE: Migratory. Breeds in Tasmania and winters in saltmarsh and grassland in coastal South Australia and Victoria. Critically endangered; only a few dozen birds remain in the wild.

VOICE: Call 'chitter-chitter'.

PSITTACULIDAE

SCARLET-CHESTED PARROT *Neophema splendida*

SIZE/ID: 20cm. Green nape, back and tail with yellow belly and bright blue face and wing-patches. Breast scarlet in male, green in female.

FOOD/BEHAVIOUR: Often forages for seeds and other plant material in low shrubs or on ground. Very quiet and easy to overlook when feeding.

HABITAT/RANGE: Dry inland areas in southern half of Australia.

VOICE: A soft twittering.

SWIFT PARROT *Lathamus discolor*

SIZE/ID: 24.5cm. Green with red patches on face, wings and tail. Red face is bordered by yellow and has blue on wings and crown.

FOOD/BEHAVIOUR: Insects, pollen, berries and nectar. Lives up to the name with fast and direct flight.

HABITAT/RANGE: Migratory. Breeds in Tasmania, winters mainly in Victoria and eastern New South Wales.

VOICE: Usually a metallic-sounding 'clink-clink' repeated quickly.

PSITTACULIDAE

AUSTRALIAN RINGNECK *Barnardius zonarius*

Port Lincoln Parrot.

Mallee Ringneck.

SIZE/ID: 37.5cm including 19cm tail. Several subspecies occur, all of which have predominantly greenish plumage with blue wings and a bold yellow collar. The two most widespread are the western Port Lincoln Parrot (*B.z. semitorquatus*), which has a black head and yellow belly, and the eastern Mallee Ringneck (*B.z. barnardi*), which has a blue-green head and red forehead,

FOOD/BEHAVIOUR: Feeds on seeds, fruits, berries, blossom, insects and larvae. Birds often inspect a variety of hollows before settling on a nest-site.

HABITAT/RANGE: Found in all mainland states, but not close to eastern or northern coasts.

VOICE: Calls include shrill 'kwink-kwink-kwink' (Mallee Ringneck) and very high-pitched whistling note repeated several times (Port Lincoln Parrot).

PSITTACULIDAE

GREEN ROSELLA *Platycercus caledonicus*

SIZE/ID: 36cm, including 17cm tail. Green-yellow head and underparts with red forehead, blue cheek, wings and tail-sides and scaly black-brown back.

FOOD/BEHAVIOUR: Often eats seeds and fruit from orchards, as well as nectar from blossom trees.

HABITAT/RANGE: Prefers woodland and eucalypt forests. Endemic to Tasmania.

VOICE: The short, shrill alarm call is often repeated a few times.

PSITTACULIDAE

CRIMSON ROSELLA *Platycercus elegans*

Crimson Rosella.

Adelaide Rosella.

SIZE/ID: 36cm, including 19cm tail. Head, underparts and rump crimson, throat, wings and tail blue and back blackish with red scaling. Subspecies *adelaidea* (known as Adelaide Rosella) has orange replacing crimson (paler in female).

FOOD/BEHAVIOUR: Diet includes wattle and eucalypt seeds. Orchard fruits are also a favourite.

HABITAT/RANGE: Open woodlands in areas of Queensland, New South Wales and Victoria. Does not venture far inland. Adelaide Rosella only found in a small area of South Australia around Murray River and Adelaide Hills.

VOICE: The quick, shrill alarm call is often repeated a few times.

PSITTACULIDAE

NORTHERN ROSELLA *Platycercus venustus*

SIZE/ID: 29cm, including 14cm tail. Black crown and shoulder, blue wings and tail, creamy underparts and rump with red undertail-coverts and mottled black and cream back.

FOOD/BEHAVIOUR: Feeds on blossom, nectar, insects and seeds gathered from savanna woodlands. Unlike other rosellas only comes to drink water at irregular intervals.

HABITAT/RANGE: Eucalypt or melaleuca forests in northern parts of Western Australia and Northern Territory.

VOICE: High-pitched disyllabic call often uttered two or three times.

PSITTACULIDAE

EASTERN ROSELLA *Platycercus eximius*

Male.

Female.

SIZE/ID: 30cm. Male has red head and breast and white throat. Belly yellow, wings and tail blue and back black with yellow scaling. Female similar to male but paler.

FOOD/BEHAVIOUR: Seeds, blossom, nectar, fruit and insects. Can cause problems in orchards.

HABITAT/RANGE: Open forest in Victoria, Tasmania, New South Wales, south-east Queensland and south-east South Australia.

VOICE: A loud 'kwink-kwink'.

PSITTACULIDAE

PALE-HEADED ROSELLA *Platycercus adscitus*

SIZE/ID: 30cm. Head white. Mantle black with yellow scaling. Wings, breast and belly blue with red vent.

FOOD/BEHAVIOUR: Feeds on grain and a variety of grass seeds.

HABITAT/RANGE: Open woodlands in parts of coastal New South Wales and Queensland.

VOICE: A loud 'kwink-kwink'.

WESTERN ROSELLA *Platycercus icterotis*

SIZE/ID: 26cm. Head and underparts red except for yellow cheek-patch. Wings and tail blue. Rump and back greenish.

FOOD/BEHAVIOUR: Grass seeds, grain and blossom. Quiet compared to other rosellas.

HABITAT/RANGE: Found only in south-west Western Australia.

VOICE: A series of whistles in quick succession.

PSITTACULIDAE

BLUE BONNET *Northiella haematogaster*

SIZE/ID: 34cm, including 17cm tail. Olive-brown overall with blue on face, wings and tail and red belly with yellowish border. Male slightly more brightly coloured than female.

FOOD/BEHAVIOUR: Seeds from various native plants like bluebush or saltbush. Often feeds on ground.

HABITAT/RANGE: Lightly timbered areas of casuarina or cypress pine in arid areas of South Australia, Victoria, New South Wales, southern Queensland and south-east Western Australia.

VOICE: Rapidly repeated harsh chattering notes when alarmed.

PSITTACULIDAE

RED-RUMPED PARROT *Psephotus haematonotus*

Male.

Female.

SIZE/ID: 27cm. Male green with yellowish belly and red patch on rump. Female mainly plain dull olive-green. Flight-feathers of both sexes tinged blue.

FOOD/BEHAVIOUR: Leaves and seeds from plants such as crowsfoot and thistles.

HABITAT/RANGE: Widespread in New South Wales and Victoria.

VOICE: Two-syllable whistle with an upward note.

PSITTACULIDAE

MULGA PARROT *Psephotus varius*

Male.

Female.

SIZE/ID: 27.5cm, including 15cm tail. Male has generally green plumage, brighter on head and breast, with yellow patches on forehead, shoulder and vent and red patches on crown, belly and rump. Female has dull yellow forehead and orange patches on crown and shoulder. Both sexes have blue on wings.

FOOD/BEHAVIOUR: Spends much of day on ground feeding on grain, grass seeds, plants and some berries. If danger approaches will fly into trees.

HABITAT/RANGE: Widespread over much of southern half of Australia. Prefers lightly timbered bush.

VOICE: Mellow flute-like call, repeated several times.

PSITTACULIDAE

GOLDEN-SHOULDERED PARROT
Psephotus chrysopterygius

SIZE/ID: 26cm. Male has turquoise head and breast, black crown and nape, red belly, olive back and tail, yellow forehead and large golden patch on shoulder. Female mostly olive-green with bluish around face, belly and tail.

FOOD/BEHAVIOUR: Feeds on a variety of native grass seeds.

HABITAT/RANGE: Considered endangered and restriced to eucalypt forests in a small area of the Cape York Peninsula, Queensland.

VOICE: A sharp metallic 'chissik-chissik'.

PSITTACULIDAE

RED-CAPPED PARROT *Purpureicephalus spurius*

SIZE/ID: 38cm. Male has red crown, nape and vent, yellow cheek, rump and upper-tail, blue underparts and wings and green back. Female more greenish in colour.

FOOD/BEHAVIOUR: Specialises on seeds from eucalypt *Corymbia calophylla*, using bill to extract seeds from hard capsules.

HABITAT/RANGE: Only found in south-west Western Australia.

VOICE: Grating 'curr-uk curr-uk'.

DOUBLE-EYED FIG PARROT *Cyclopsitta diophthalma*

SIZE/ID: 15cm. Short-tailed. Mainly green with variable red and blue markings on crown and cheek. Wings blue.

FOOD/BEHAVIOUR: Native figs and seeds of tropical fruit. Often sits quietly among foliage.

HABITAT/RANGE: Only found in a few small areas of Queensland and New South Wales, mainly near coast.

VOICE: Shrill, penetrating 'tseet-tseet-tseet'.

PSITTACULIDAE

BUDGERIGAR *Melopsittacus undulatus*

SIZE/ID: 18cm, including 9.5cm tail. Back of crown, neck, nape, back and wings finely barred brown and yellow. Tail-feathers pale green-blue. Underparts pale green.

FOOD/BEHAVIOUR: Feeds on ground, mostly on grass seeds.

HABITAT/RANGE: Range extends over most of Australia, particularly in the interior. Highly nomadic, travelling to wherever there is an abundance of food and water.

VOICE: A pleasant, chattering warble.

PSITTACULIDAE

MUSK LORIKEET *Glossopsitta concinna*

SIZE/ID: 22cm. Mostly green with red forehead and ear-coverts, blue patch on crown, yellow patch on side of breast and brown-bronze nape.

FOOD/BEHAVIOUR: Mainly pollen, blossoms and insects. Can become so engaged in feeding that they pay no attention to any form of danger.

HABITAT/RANGE: Forests from south-east South Australia through Victoria and New South Wales to south-east Queensland, also in eastern Tasmania.

VOICE: Utters a shrill screech, and when feeding continued chattering.

PSITTACULIDAE

LITTLE LORIKEET *Glossopsitta pusilla*

SIZE/ID: 15.5cm. Plumage green, paler on breast, with red forehead and throat. Nape and upper back brownish.

FOOD/BEHAVIOUR: Pollen, nectar, blossom, both native and cultivated fruits and a variety of seeds. When feeding on blossom trees these birds are fearless and pay little attention to humans.

HABITAT/RANGE: Areas not far from coast in Victoria and New South Wales. Range extends to south-east South Australia and south-east Queensland.

VOICE: A shrill screech.

PSITTACULIDAE

PURPLE-CROWNED LORIKEET
Glossopsitta porphyrocephala

SIZE/ID: 16cm. Mostly green with orange-yellow cheek-spot and forehead, red on lores and purple crown. Throat and breast pale blue and mantle brownish.

FOOD/BEHAVIOUR: Feeds on flowering eucalypts, nectar, blossom and a variety of fruits, particularly cultivated fruits. It is not uncommon for these birds to nest in colonies.

HABITAT/RANGE: Woodland and scrub in areas of Western Australia, South Australia and Victoria.

VOICE: A rapid shrill 'tsit-tsit-tsit'.

PSITTACULIDAE

RAINBOW LORIKEET *Trichoglossus haematodus*

SIZE/ID: 23cm. Green with blue head and belly, orange-red breast and yellow collar.

FOOD/BEHAVIOUR: Pollen, nectar, blossom, fruit, seeds and insects. Sunrise sees mass departure of roosting birds to feeding grounds.

HABITAT/RANGE: Woodlands in Western Australia, South Australia, Victoria, New South Wales and Queensland.

VOICE: A shrill chatter when feeding.

MENURIDAE

SUPERB LYREBIRD *Menura novaehollandiae*

SIZE/ID: 98cm, including tail of up to 55cm. Female smaller than male. Plumage grey-brown overall, with rufous throat. Tail long in both sexes but that of male is barred and has spectacular plumes which are raised during display.

FOOD/BEHAVIOUR: Small creatures such as worms or grubs are dug from logs or the ground.

HABITAT/RANGE: Prefers rainforest areas of eastern Victoria, eastern New South Wales and small areas of south-east Queensland and central Tasmania.

VOICE: Amazing song mimics sounds of the forest, including song of almost any other bird. Calls include low-pitched 'chuck' and high-pitched shriek.

PTILONORHYNCHIDAE

REGENT BOWERBIRD *Sericulus chrysocephalus*

Male.

Female.

SIZE/ID: 27cm. Male black with yellow crown, nape and wing-patch and top of crown tinged orange. Female brown with pale scalloping and black patches on crown and throat.

FOOD/BEHAVIOUR: Fruits, leaves and insects. Adult male has spectacular display.

HABITAT/RANGE: Only in rainforests in eastern New South Wales and Queensland.

VOICE: Churring squawk.

PTILONORHYNCHIDAE

SATIN BOWERBIRD *Ptilonorhynchus violaceus*

Male.

Female.

SIZE/ID: 33cm. Adult male blackish with purple sheen. Grey-green female scaly on underparts. Both sexes have purple eye.

FOOD/BEHAVIOUR: Fruits, other plant matter and invertebrates. Male fills display bower with blue objects.

HABITAT/RANGE: Rainforest and other habitats in Victoria, New South Wales and Queensland.

VOICE: A harsh wheezing call.

PTILONORHYNCHIDAE

SPOTTED BOWERBIRD *Ptilonorhynchus maculatus*

SIZE/ID: 31cm. Neck and head speckled fawn-brown, grey nape with lilac-pink tuft, back dark brown and heavily marked with bold buff spots and crescents.

FOOD/BEHAVIOUR: Feeds on berries and both cultivated and native fruits. Considered by some to be the most gifted of all the bower-builders; male fills bower with white objects.

HABITAT/RANGE: Arid scrub and dry woodland in parts of New South Wales and Queensland.

VOICE: A penetrating drawn-out rasping note.

CLIMACTERIDAE

WHITE-THROATED TREECREEPER
Cormobates leucophaea

SIZE/ID: 17cm. Dark olive-brown above with pale flash on wing. Throat and breast white, feathers on flanks edged with brown. Female has rufous spot on ear-covert.

FOOD/BEHAVIOUR: Feeds on a variety of insects and other invertebrates. Climbs trees in a very unusual way, with one foot always in front of the other; all treecreepers do the same thing.

HABITAT/RANGE: Occurs in forests from south-east South Australia through Victoria and eastern New South Wales and into eastern Queensland.

VOICE: Either a shrill whistle or harsh chattering.

CLIMACTERIDAE

BROWN TREECREEPER *Climacteris picumnus*

SIZE/ID: 18cm. Fairly plain grey-brown on upperparts, with dark brown and buff streaking on belly and flanks. Has dark eye-stripe and broad pale supercilium. Female has diffuse rufous spot on upper breast.

FOOD/BEHAVIOUR: Invertebrates of any type make up bulk of diet. Forages mainly on tree trunks, under bark and cracks or crevices on limbs. Will vigorously defend territory against other birds, often chasing them away.

HABITAT/RANGE: Found in any type of woodland throughout most of Queensland, New South Wales and Victoria, and also in eastern South Australia.

VOICE: Series of sharp, hard whistles with only one pitch.

MALURIDAE

SUPERB FAIRY-WREN *Malurus cyaneus*

Male.

Female.

SIZE/ID: 16cm. Breeding male has blue patches on crown, cheek and back. Eye-stripe, throat, and tail blackish. Female and immature pale brown with rufous bill, face and legs.

FOOD/BEHAVIOUR: Feeds on insects. Immatures help adults to feed new chicks.

HABITAT/RANGE: Forest, scrub and gardens in Tasmania, Victoria, New South Wales, south-east South Australia and south-east Queensland.

VOICE: A low churring note.

MELIPHAGIDAE

YELLOW-SPOTTED HONEYEATER
Meliphaga notata

SIZE/ID: 18cm. Mostly olive-green with yellow gape and yellow patch on ear-covert which forms a rounded triangle (very similar and more widespread Lewin's Honeyeater has larger crescent-shape on ear and machine-gun-like call).

FOOD/BEHAVIOUR: Diet mainly insects and nectar. Very fond of lantana berries and most blossom trees. One of the most agressive species of honeyeater.

HABITAT/RANGE: Coastal area of Queensland, mainly north of Townsville in the tropical rainforest region.

VOICE: Harsh call like 'tchu-chua'.

MELIPHAGIDAE

YELLOW-FACED HONEYEATER
Lichenostomus chrysops

SIZE/ID: 17cm. Yellow stripe under eye bordered above and below with black and ending in a small white tuft. Rest of bird mainly grey-brown, with olive-green wash on wings.

FOOD/BEHAVIOUR: Feeds on nectar and a variety of small insects.

HABITAT/RANGE: Found in a variety of bush and woodland from south-east South Australia through Victoria and into eastern New South Wales and Queensland.

VOICE: Call is a loud 'chik-up chik-up chik-up'.

MELIPHAGIDAE

SINGING HONEYEATER *Lichenostomus virescens*

SIZE/ID: 19cm. Mainly pale grey-brown with wing- and tail-feathers edged olive-green. Breast paler and streaked grey. Broad blackish stripe through eye to side of neck bordered below by narrower yellow stripe.

FOOD/BEHAVIOUR: Nectar, fruit, spiders and insects such as moths and beetles. One of the most agressive species of honeyeaters.

HABITAT/RANGE: Found over most of the mainland but not along the east coast or in Tasmania.

VOICE: Song loud and varied, but not very tuneful.

MELIPHAGIDAE

WHITE-EARED HONEYEATER
Lichenostomus leucotis

SIZE/ID: 20cm. Plumage bright olive-green with grey crown, black face and throat and prominent white ear-patch.

FOOD/BEHAVIOUR: Gleans insects from leaves of trees and also gathers sap from some eucalypts.

HABITAT/RANGE: Prefers heaths, mallee woodlands and moist areas across southern regions from south-west Western Australia through South Australia, Victoria and New South Wales and north through eastern Queensland.

VOICE: Loud ringing 'chock-chop, cherry-bob cher-up'.

MELIPHAGIDAE

YELLOW-TUFTED HONEYEATER
Lichenostomus melanops

SIZE/ID: 23cm. Head mainly yellow with large black mask. Rest of bird, including underparts, back and wings, shades of grey to olive. Image shows rare subspecies *cassides* (known as Helmeted Honeyeater), which has bulbous yellow crown and occurs only in a small area near Melbourne.

FOOD/BEHAVIOUR: Feeds on small scale insects gathered in trees or from under bark.

HABITAT/RANGE: Woodland in south-east South Australia, Victoria, eastern New South Wales and south-east Queensland.

VOICE: Loud 'tchurr-tchurr'.

MELIPHAGIDAE

YELLOW-PLUMED HONEYEATER
Lichenostomus ornatus

SIZE/ID: 18cm. Underparts streaked grey, upperparts grey-brown, wings and head yellow-green. Has narrow yellow stripe under eye and yellow plume on each side of neck.

FOOD/BEHAVIOUR: Feeds on insects gleaned from leaves, and on eucalypt trees.

HABITAT/RANGE: Mallee, mulga and savanna woodlands in southern parts of Western Australia and South Australia and western areas of Victoria and New South Wales.

VOICE: Harsh 'chick-o-wee chick-o-wee'.

MELIPHAGIDAE

NOISY MINER *Manorina melanocephala*

SIZE/ID: 28cm. Mottled grey-brown overall with black crown and cheek, whitish forehead and face, olive-green patch on wing and yellow legs, bill and patch of skin behind eye.

FOOD/BEHAVIOUR: Insects and other small invertebrates. During nesting season up to 20 birds have been known to help feed one brood.

HABITAT/RANGE: Woodlands and parks from south-east South Australia and Tasmania through Victoria and New South Wales to eastern Queensland.

VOICE: A complicated repertoire. Common calls include 'teu-teu-teu-teu'.

MELIPHAGIDAE

RED WATTLEBIRD *Anthochaera carunculata*

SIZE/ID: 35cm. Large with long tail and decurved bill. Brown with heavy white streaking, yellow belly and small red wattle below ear.

FOOD/BEHAVIOUR: Noisy acrobatic bird which feeds on spiders, insects and nectar from native plants such as banksias.

HABITAT/RANGE: Woodland, parks and gardens in southern parts of Western Australia and South Australia, Victoria, eastern New South Wales and south-east Queensland.

VOICE: Call 'tobacco-box tobacco-box'.

MELIPHAGIDAE

TAWNY-CROWNED HONEYEATER
Glyciphila melanops

SIZE/ID: 16cm. Upperparts pale brown with streaking. Head has tawny crown, white throat and supercilium and black eye-stripe which continues down side of breast.

FOOD/BEHAVIOUR: Feeds on a variety of insects and nectar from banksias, grevilleas and flowering gums. Also gathers blossom from a variety of trees and shrubs.

HABITAT/RANGE: Coastal regions of Western Australia, South Australia, Victoria, New South Wales and Tasmania. Prefers the heathlands and some mallee scrub.

VOICE: Pleasant flute-like call.

MELIPHAGIDAE

NEW HOLLAND HONEYEATER
Phylidonyris novaehollandiae

SIZE/ID: 18cm. Boldly marked black and white, with decurved bill, white eye and bright golden-yellow patches on wings and tail.

FOOD/BEHAVIOUR: Diet includes nectar and insects. One of few birds that can catch and hold more than one insect in its bill (it can hold up to four).

HABITAT/RANGE: Often seen in coastal heath in south-west Western Australia, south-east South Australia, Victoria, Tasmania, New South Wales and south-east Queensland.

VOICE: Loud 'tchlik-tchlik-tchlik', plus a weak whistle.

MELIPHAGIDAE

WHITE-NAPED HONEYEATER *Melithreptus lunatus*

SIZE/ID: 14cm. Head black with white throat, white patch on nape and small red wattle over eye. Back, rump and tail bright olive, underparts white.

FOOD/BEHAVIOUR: Nectar, pollen and invertebrates make up bulk of diet; also honeydew gathered from eucalypt leaves.

HABITAT/RANGE: Wet and dry forests from south-east South Australia through Victoria and New South Wales and into eastern Queensland.

VOICE: A sharp and grating call, also 'tsit-tsit-tsit'.

MELIPHAGIDAE

BLUE-FACED HONEYEATER *Entomyzon cyanoyis*

SIZE/ID: 30cm. Head and throat black with blue skin around eye (green in young birds) and white moustache. Upperparts olive-yellow, underparts white.

FOOD/BEHAVIOUR: Like most honeyeaters diet includes nectar, insects, pollen and fruit. In banana-growing areas it is called the 'banana bird'.

HABITAT/RANGE: Range extends from north of Western Australia east to Queensland and then south to New South Wales, Victoria and south-east South Australia. Absent from inland areas and Tasmania.

VOICE: Calls include 'mew-ky-owt' and 'teeu-teeu'.

MELIPHAGIDAE

CRIMSON CHAT *Epthianura tricolor*

Male.

Female.

SIZE/ID: 12cm. Male has red crown, breast and rump, white throat and brown back. Female buff-brown with red on underparts and rump.

FOOD/BEHAVIOUR: Insects and some nectar. Partly nomadic in search of suitable breeding conditions.

HABITAT/RANGE: Occurs Australia-wide except north and east coasts. Favours inland plains and saltbush.

VOICE: A high chiming 'swee-swee-swee'.

MELIPHAGIDAE

ORANGE CHAT *Epthianura aurifrons*

Male.

Female.

SIZE/ID: 12cm. Male yellow with black face and throat and tinged with orange on crown and breast. Blackish tail tipped white. Female pale yellowish-brown; red eye distinguishes it from similar Yellow Chat.

FOOD/BEHAVIOUR: Insects and some nectar. Usually nests in colonies.

HABITAT/RANGE: Nomadic. Widespread, favouring arid inland areas such as saltbush plains, gibber country and salt lakes.

VOICE: Metallic 'tang' and 'cheek-cheek-cheek'.

MELIPHAGIDAE

WHITE-FRONTED CHAT *Epthianura albifrons*

Male.

Female.

SIZE/ID: 13cm. Male has white head and throat, black rear-crown, collar and breast-band, grey back and white belly. Female grey-brown with white face and throat and dark breast-band.

FOOD/BEHAVIOUR: Insects. Often nests around swamps and lakes.

HABITAT/RANGE: Plains and grasslands in south Western Australia, South Australia, New South Wales, Victoria and Tasmania.

VOICE: A sharp nasal squeak.

DASYORNITHIDAE

RUFOUS BRISTLEBIRD *Dasyornis broadbenti*

SIZE/ID: 27cm. Upperparts grey-brown to cinnamon, wings and tail darker. Crown and cheeks brighter rufous. Throat and lores whitish. Breast speckled grey-brown.

FOOD/BEHAVIOUR: Berries, beetles, worms and grubs. Often prefers to run rather than fly.

HABITAT/RANGE: Only in a small area of grassland in coastal western Victoria. Small population in Western Australia considered extinct.

VOICE: Harsh 'tweek' alarm-call and a repeated 'chip-chop chip-chop'.

PARDALOTIDAE

SPOTTED PARDALOTE *Pardalotus punctatus*

Male.

Female.

SIZE/ID: 9cm. Tiny with pale supercilium and bold white spots on upperparts. Has black crown, wings and tail, brown mantle, red rump and yellow undertail. Male has greyish cheeks and breast-sides and yellow throat.

FOOD/BEHAVIOUR: Invertebrates. Digs a nest-burrow up to 60cm long in a creek bank.

HABITAT/RANGE: Along south coast from south-west Western Australia to Tasmania and Victoria, and north through New South Wales to north-east Queensland.

VOICE: Soft 'pee-too' and also 'sleep-bab-eeee'.

PARDALOTIDAE

STRIATED PARDALOTE *Pardalotus striatus*

SIZE/ID: 11cm. Crown, eye-stripe, wings and tail blackish with variable white streaking. Mantle brown and supercilium and underparts yellow and white.

FOOD/BEHAVIOUR: Feeds on insects such as cicadas, beetles, ants, caterpillars and grubs.

HABITAT/RANGE: Found in forests Australia-wide, including in Tasmania.

VOICE: Sharp 'pick-it-up' and a 'chip-chip' call.

ACANTHIZIDAE

WHITE-BROWED SCRUBWREN *Sericornis frontalis*

SIZE/ID: 14cm. Brown upperparts, rufous tail, yellow eye and dark mask bordered by white supercilium and white moustache.

FOOD/BEHAVIOUR: Feeds on a variety of insects, including flies and caterpillars, and other creatures. Usually seen on or close to the ground.

HABITAT/RANGE: Forests along southern and eastern coasts, from south-west Western Australia east to Victoria and Tasmania and north to New South Wales and Queensland.

VOICE: Rapid 'tsi-tsi-tsi-tsi'.

ACANTHIZIDAE

BUFF-RUMPED THORNBILL *Acanthiza reguloides*

SIZE/ID: 11cm. Plumage mainly plain olive-brown above and paler on underparts. White eye. Rump, upper-tail and tail-tip pale buff and has pale flecking on head and neck.

FOOD/BEHAVIOUR: Diet mainly insects and other small creatures. Feeds on ground and in trees.

HABITAT/RANGE: Prefers open forest and woodland country. Range extends from south-east South Australia through Victoria and New South Wales to eastern Queensland.

VOICE: Often a quiet note, but when alarmed call becomes louder and louder.

ACANTHIZIDAE

BROWN THORNBILL *Acanthiza pusilla*

SIZE/ID: 10cm. Plain olive-brown above and buff below, with red eye, rufous on forehead and rump and brown streaking on breast.

FOOD/BEHAVIOUR: Prefers invertebrates such as caterpillars and spiders. Often feeds in low-growing shrubs. Nest built of grass and usually very large and untidy, often close to ground in a shrub.

HABITAT/RANGE: Woodlands, parks and gardens in south-east Queensland, New South Wales, Victoria, Tasmania and south-east South Australia.

VOICE: Harsh churring call.

ACANTHIZIDAE

YELLOW-RUMPED THORNBILL
Acanthiza chrysorrhoa

SIZE/ID: 11cm. Black forehead spotted with white, black tail and yellow rump. Upperparts olive-brown, underparts buff.

FOOD/BEHAVIOUR: Diet includes insects, spiders and grass seeds. Nomadic outside breeding season.

HABITAT/RANGE: Found over much of Australia, including Tasmania, although absent from far north. Prefers open forest and gardens.

VOICE: Sharp repeated 'zip-zip-zip'.

ACANTHIZIDAE

STRIATED THORNBILL *Acanthiza lineata*

SIZE/ID: 10cm. Head, wings and tail dull olive-brown. Head has white streaking and tail a dark subterminal band. Underparts whitish with brown streaks on breast and a touch of yellow on belly.

FOOD/BEHAVIOUR: Feeds mainly on spiders and insects. A common bird, but not often seen as they feed high in trees. Records show that the average lifespan for many thornbills is one year.

HABITAT/RANGE: Prefers wet, open forests and mountain country from south-east South Australia, through Victoria and New South Wales and into south-east Queensland.

VOICE: A soft 'zit-zit-zit'.

ACANTHIZIDAE

WEEBILL *Smicrornis brevirostris*

SIZE/ID: 9cm. The smallest bird in Australia. Upperparts and head olive-brown, underparts pale buff with pale eye and supercilium. Bill short and stumpy compared to thornbills.

FOOD/BEHAVIOUR: Feeds in trees, moving from limb to limb in search of small insects and larvae. Builds a very neat and tidy pear-shaped nest.

HABITAT/RANGE: Occurs over most of mainland Australia, wherever suitable forests or woodlands are found.

VOICE: A sharp repeated 'chiz-chiz-chiz'.

POMATOSTOMIDAE

WHITE-BROWED BABBLER
Pomatostomus superciliosus

SIZE/ID: 20cm. Long decurved bill and long tail. Head, upperparts, flanks and belly dark grey. Supercilium, throat, breast and corners of tail white.

FOOD/BEHAVIOUR: Feeds on insects, spiders and similar creatures. Lives in groups of up to ten birds. Defends territory all year round.

HABITAT/RANGE: Dry bush and woodland areas in the southern half of Australia, but absent from Tasmania.

VOICE: Repeated call 'tuk-tuk-tuk-tuk'.

ARTAMIDAE

WHITE-BROWED WOODSWALLOW
Artamus superciliosus

SIZE/ID: 19cm. Grey head, breast and upperparts, belly rufous, supercilium and tail-tip white. Female paler than male.

FOOD/BEHAVIOUR: Catches insects such as flies and locusts on the wing.

HABITAT/RANGE: Occurs almost Australia-wide, but not in Tasmania. Highly nomadic.

VOICE: Alarm a frequent hard chatter.

WHITE-BREASTED WOODSWALLOW
Artamus leucorhynchus

SIZE/ID: 17cm. Dark brown on head, throat, upperparts and tail, with white belly and rump.

FOOD/BEHAVIOUR: Catches flying insects on wing. Highly nomadic. Often in flocks.

HABITAT/RANGE: Occurs Australia-wide except Tasmania.

VOICE: A nasal chirping.

ARTAMIDAE

DUSKY WOODSWALLOW *Artamus cyanopterus*

SIZE/ID: 18cm. Dark greyish overall, with wings blue-grey. Wing-feathers have narrow white edges and tail-corners tipped white.

FOOD/BEHAVIOUR: Feeds on small invertebrates. Small nest, situated up to 4m off ground, is built of grass and twigs. Several birds often huddle next to each other on a branch.

HABITAT/RANGE: From south-west Western Australia east to Victoria and north to eastern Queensland.

VOICE: A vigorous harassing call.

CRACTICIDAE

GREY BUTCHERBIRD *Cracticus torquatus*

SIZE/ID: 32cm. Head, crown and back mostly black, with white throat, underparts, neck-sides and rump. Mantle grey and has white markings on wing and on corners of tail.

FOOD/BEHAVIOUR: Small reptiles, insects, mice, small birds and some fruits. Name comes from habit of impaling prey on a branch or spine.

HABITAT/RANGE: Common in areas of open woodland all over Australia, except in the far north.

VOICE: Has a very pleasant call with loud whistling notes, also mimics other birds.

CRACTICIDAE

PIED BUTCHERBIRD *Cracticus nigrogularis*

SIZE/ID: 35cm. Black head and upperparts, white underparts, collar, wing-bars, rump and tail-corners.

FOOD/BEHAVIOUR: Rodents, birds and lizards. Often impales prey on a branch.

HABITAT/RANGE: A variety of habitats over most of Australia, but absent from south coast and Tasmania.

VOICE: Loud flute-like song, alarm call is a loud shriek.

AUSTRALIAN MAGPIE *Cracticus tibicen*

SIZE/ID: 44cm. Black with white nape, undertail-coverts and tail-base and variable amounts of white on upperparts.

FOOD/BEHAVIOUR: Invertebrates, small animals and birds. Chicks leave nest before they can fly and parents feed them on ground.

HABITAT/RANGE: Occurs Australia-wide in a variety of habitats.

VOICE: Loud flute-like song with whistling notes.

CRACTICIDAE

PIED CURRAWONG *Strepera graculina*

SIZE/ID: 46cm. A very robust bird with a stout bill. Plumage nearly all black, with white wing-patches and white on rump, base of tail and tip of tail. Eye yellow.

FOOD/BEHAVIOUR: Feeds on small birds and animals, insects and fruits. During winter commonly frequents cities in search of food scraps.

HABITAT/RANGE: Found along eastern coast of Australia, in Victoria, New South Wales and Queensland, and for a few hundred kilometres inland.

VOICE: Double call of 'curra-wong curra-wong'.

CAMPEPHAGIDAE

BLACK-FACED CUCKOOSHRIKE
Coracina novaehollandiae

SIZE/ID: 33cm. Pale blue-grey overall, with forehead, face and throat black. Belly whitish and wing-tips and tail-feathers almost black.

FOOD/BEHAVIOUR: Mainly feeds on a variety of insects. Very selective when choosing a nest site, with both male and female going to great trouble to find the correct limb.

HABITAT/RANGE: Found in all types of woodland all over Australia, including Tasmania.

VOICE: Call a pleasant 'chereer-chereer'.

PACHYCEPHALIDAE

GREY SHRIKE-THRUSH *Colluricincla harmonica*

SIZE/ID: 22.5cm. Most of upperparts grey-brown, with mantle brown. Underparts pale grey, female with finely streaked throat, male plain. Lores white.

FOOD/BEHAVIOUR: Insects, lizards and mammals, sometimes robs other nests of young. Often forages around old trees or tree stumps.

HABITAT/RANGE: Range covers almost all of Australia and Tasmania. Found in all types of woodland.

VOICE: Very clear and melodious call is running whistle 'whit-whit-whit-whit'.

PACHYCEPHALIDAE

GOLDEN WHISTLER *Pachycephala pectoralis*

Male.

Female.

SIZE/ID: 17cm. Male's head black with white throat bordered by narrow black breast-band, yellow underparts and upperparts olive-green and grey. Female plain olive-grey with paler throat and some yellow on underparts.

FOOD/BEHAVIOUR: Hunts in trees for insects and their larvae. Often seen in pairs.

HABITAT/RANGE: Forest and woodland along south and east coasts, from south-west Western Australia through South Australia, Victoria, Tasmania, New South Wales and Queensland.

VOICE: Best known is 'chee-chee-chee'.

PACHYCEPHALIDAE

RUFOUS WHISTLER *Pachycephala rufiventris*

Male.

Female.

SIZE/ID: 17cm. Upperparts and crown olive-grey. Male has rufous underparts and black mask and breast-band bordering white throat. Female buff underneath with fine streaking.

FOOD/BEHAVIOUR: Catches insects among tree branches. Also feeds on fruit. Partly nomadic.

HABITAT/RANGE: Austalia-wide except Tasmania in all types of forest and woodland.

VOICE: Often gives a 'pee-pee joey-joey-joey'.

ORIOLIDAE

OLIVE-BACKED ORIOLE *Oriolus sagittatus*

SIZE/ID: 28cm. Head and mantle olive-green. Tail- and wing-feathers mainly grey with white tips. Underparts white with dark streaking. Bill and eye reddish.

FOOD/BEHAVIOUR: Diet mainly native fruits and berries, but also known to catch insects on the wing.

HABITAT/RANGE: Forest areas from south-east South Australia through Victoria, New South Wales, Queensland, Northern Territory into northern Western Australia. Range does not extend more than a few hundred kilometres from the coast.

VOICE: Low-pitched 'orry-orry-oo' and also mimics other birds.

ORIOLIDAE

AUSTRALIAN FIGBIRD *Sphecotheres vieilloti*

Male.

Female.

SIZE/ID: 28cm. Male has glossy black head with bare red skin around eye, grey neck, olive-green upperparts and black tail with white tips. Female has olive-brown upperparts with dark streaks on head and white underparts with heavy dark brown streaking.

FOOD/BEHAVIOUR: Feeds on a variety of fruit, both native and cultivated.

HABITAT/RANGE: Occurs mainly along the coasts of New South Wales, Queensland, Northern Territory and north Western Australia.

VOICE: Chatters like a parrot and gives a loud 'scluck'.

RHIPIDURIDAE

WILLIE-WAGTAIL *Rhipidura leucophrys*

SIZE/ID: 20cm. Long fan-shaped tail. Plumage mainly black with white eyebrow and underparts.

FOOD/BEHAVIOUR: Forages on the wing or on the ground for insects, spiders and worms. Fearless and confiding and will chase after almost any other bird.

HABITAT/RANGE: Found all over Australia in a variety of woodland areas. Frequently seen in parks and gardens.

VOICE: Song resembles 'sweet pretty creature'.

GREY FANTAIL *Rhipidura albiscapa*

SIZE/ID: 16cm. Grey overall with buff underparts and white throat, supercilium, wing-bars and tips to long tail-feathers.

FOOD/BEHAVIOUR: Feeds mainly on flying insects. Very easy to identify because often fans tail. Nest is also a well-built structure with a 'wine glass stem' attached.

HABITAT/RANGE: Found all over Australia and Tasmania in a wide variety of habitats.

VOICE: High-pitched melodious song, call often a sharp 'chip-chip'.

RHIPIDURIDAE

RUFOUS FANTAIL *Rhipidura rufifrons*

SIZE/ID: 16cm. Upperparts brown with rufous forehead and rump. Long fan-shaped tail has white tip. Underparts buff with dark speckles on breast.

FOOD/BEHAVIOUR: Catches insects such as moths and flies on the wing. Like the Grey Fantail builds a 'wine glass stem' on the nest, although as yet no one has been able to explain the purpose of this structure.

HABITAT/RANGE: Coastal areas of Victoria, New South Wales and Queensland. Often seen in heavy undergrowth, especially in areas close to water.

VOICE: A single 'chip'.

MONARCHIDAE

MAGPIE-LARK *Grallina cyanoleuca*

SIZE/ID: 27cm. Black throat, crown and wings, with white patches on face, white wing-patches and white tail with black patch. Male has white supercilium, female white face.

FOOD/BEHAVIOUR: Feeds on a variety of insects. Builds a cup-shaped nest out of mud.

HABITAT/RANGE: Occurs Australia-wide in a range of habitats, but not in dense forest.

VOICE: A distinctive 'pee-o-wee'.

MONARCHIDAE

SATIN FLYCATCHER *Myiagra cyanoleuca*

Male.

Female.

SIZE/ID: 16cm. Both sexes have erectile crest. Male has upperparts, head, throat and breast glossy black, belly and flanks white. Female has blue-grey head and mantle with rufous throat, white underparts and brown wings and tail.

FOOD/BEHAVIOUR: Catches insects on the wing. Very active.

HABITAT/RANGE: Wet forest areas, including valleys and low mountains, along east coast from Queensland to Victoria and Tasmania.

VOICE: Song a loud whistle-like 'choo-ee choo-ee'.

CORVIDAE

LITTLE RAVEN *Corvus mellori*

SIZE/ID: 50cm. Uniform glossy black with pale eye.

FOOD/BEHAVIOUR: Carrion, insects and sometimes grain. Breeding season variable; in mountain areas from December, in lowlands from August.

HABITAT/RANGE: Most of Victoria and New South Wales and a small area of south-east South Australia.

VOICE: A guttural 'ark-ark-ark'.

PETROICIDAE

JACKY WINTER *Microeca fascinans*

SIZE/ID: 13cm. Grey-brown upperparts, underparts off-white. Has dark lores, a white supercilium and broad white outer tail-feathers.

FOOD/BEHAVIOUR: Feeds on a variety of invertebrates and many other small creatures.

HABITAT/RANGE: Prefers dry open forest, woodland and mallee, also found in cultivated and grazing areas. Occurs across the Australian mainland but not in Tasmania. A common bird in some areas.

VOICE: A high whistling note, repeated several times.

PETROICIDAE

SCARLET ROBIN *Petroica boodang*

Male.

Female.

SIZE/ID: 13cm. Both sexes have white forehead and red breast. Male black on head and upperparts with white wing-bars and outer tail-feathers. Female mainly brown with a duller red breast and smaller white markings on wing.

FOOD/BEHAVIOUR: Insects and other invertebrates. The cup-shaped nest is beautifully built.

HABITAT/RANGE: Woodlands in south-west Western Australia and from south-east South Australia through Victoria, Tasmania and New South Wales to south-east Queensland.

VOICE: A succession of low trilling notes.

PETROICIDAE

RED-CAPPED ROBIN *Petroica goodenovii*

Male.

Female.

SIZE/ID: 11.5cm. Male has red cap and breast. Head and upperparts mainly black with bold white wing-bars and tail-edges. Female dull grey-brown with buff-white markings in wing and outer-tail, reddish forehead and pink to pale brown breast.

FOOD/BEHAVIOUR: Invertebrates. Expert at broken-wing act to lure predators away from nest.

HABITAT/RANGE: Drier woodlands over most of Australia, except for Tasmania and tropical wet areas.

VOICE: A staccato rattling song, repeated several times.

PETROICIDAE

HOODED ROBIN *Melanodryas cucullata*

SIZE/ID: 17cm. Both sexes have white patches on wing and tail-sides. Male has black head, breast, wings and tail with white patch on shoulder. Female mostly plain pale grey, darker on wings and tail.

FOOD/BEHAVIOUR: Insects and worms. Expert at performing broken-wing act to distract predators from nest.

HABITAT/RANGE: Australia-wide except Tasmania and east Queensland.

VOICE: A penetrating whistle with chattering notes.

EASTERN YELLOW ROBIN *Eopsaltria australis*

SIZE/ID: 15cm. Adult grey above with yellow underparts and rump. Juvenile dark brown with whitish streaking.

FOOD/BEHAVIOUR: Insects and other invertebrates.

HABITAT/RANGE: Wetter regions in south-east South Australia, Victoria, New South Wales and Queensland.

VOICE: A range of piping notes.

HIRUNDINIDAE

WELCOME SWALLOW *Hirundo neoxena*

SIZE/ID: 15cm. Glossy dark blue above with orange-red forehead and throat and pale grey underparts. Forked tail has long streamers and white spots at base.

FOOD/BEHAVIOUR: Takes flying insects on the wing. Builds a cup-shaped nest using mud.

HABITAT/RANGE: Occurs Australia-wide, although less common in the arid inland regions.

VOICE: A pleasant twittering song.

ACROCEPHALIDAE

AUSTRALIAN REED-WARBLER
Acrocephalus australis

SIZE/ID: 17cm. Upperparts fairly plain olive-brown. Underparts mainly buff, being paler on throat and darker on flanks. Pale supercilium does not extend far behind eye. Tail rounded at tip.

FOOD/BEHAVIOUR: Feeds on insects and small animals. Nest is a cup of reeds and straw attached to upright reeds and suspended over water.

HABITAT/RANGE: Usually associated with reedbeds around pools or other bodies of water. Occurs Australia-wide, including in Tasmania.

VOICE: Distinctive song repeats a variety of notes such as 'crut-crut-crut-crut' and 'deet-deet-deet'.

CISTICOLIDAE

GOLDEN-HEADED CISTICOLA *Cisticola exilis*

SIZE/ID: 10cm. Upperparts pale brown with dark streaking, rump rufous and tail brown. Underparts, throat and cheek pale buff. Crown golden-orange, unmarked in breeding male and streaked in all other plumages.

FOOD/BEHAVIOUR: Insects and their larvae form bulk of diet. Males perch on rushes and limbs calling incessantly and then drop to cover.

HABITAT/RANGE: Grasslands from north of Western Australia east through Northern Territory and Queensland and south to New South Wales, Victoria and just into South Australia.

VOICE: A persistent grating 'zzzt, zzzt' call.

ZOSTEROPIDAE

SILVEREYE *Zosterops lateralis*

SIZE/ID: 12cm. Yellow-green head, wings and tail. Grey mantle and underparts. Bold white eye-ring. Birds which breed in Tasmania have rufous flanks.

FOOD/BEHAVIOUR: Feeds on insects and other invertebrates.

HABITAT/RANGE: Woodlands from south-west Western Australia through South Australia, Victoria, Tasmania, New South Wales and eastern Queensland.

VOICE: Warbling song and 'see' call.

TURDIDAE

BASSIAN THRUSH *Zoothera lunulata*

SIZE/ID: 26cm. Upperparts brown, underparts white. Heavily barred all over body with dark brown crescents. Head speckled with plain white lores. Tail and wings dark brown.

FOOD/BEHAVIOUR: Worms and insects gathered from the forest floor. If seen will just freeze in position using the body colours as camouflage.

HABITAT/RANGE: Forests and woodlands along the east coast of Australia from South Australia to Queensland, including Tasmania.

VOICE: Often quiet, but call 'seep' and song a tuneful warble.

DICAEIDAE

MISTLETOEBIRD *Dicaeum hirundinaceum*

Male.

Female.

SIZE/ID: 11cm. Male has black upperparts, grey flanks and red throat, breast and undertail-coverts. Female dark grey-brown above, pale greyish below with pink undertail-coverts.

FOOD/BEHAVIOUR: Feeds mainly on mistletoe berries, insects and a variety of seeds and berries from other native trees.

HABITAT/RANGE: Occurs over all of Australia except Tasmania. Found in all types of forests and woodlands.

VOICE: High-pitched 'wita-wita' call.

ESTRILDIDAE

DIAMOND FIRETAIL *Stagonopleura guttata*

SIZE/ID: 12cm. Black lores, tail and breast-band. Flanks black with diamond spots. Head grey, back and wings grey-brown, throat and belly white. Bill, eye and rump bright red.

FOOD/BEHAVIOUR: Insects and grass seeds. Very social, often seen in flocks.

HABITAT/RANGE: Grasslands and lightly timbered areas from south-east South Australia through Victoria and New South Wales to south-east Queensland.

VOICE: Drawn-out and plaintive 'twoo-twoo-twoo'.

ESTRILDIDAE

RED-BROWED FINCH *Neochmia temporalis*

SIZE/ID: 12cm. Bill, lores, supercilium and rump crimson. Head and underparts grey. Upperparts olive-green, brighter around nape. Tail black.

FOOD/BEHAVIOUR: Feeds on a variety of ripe grasses, berries and insects. Prior to mating the displaying male holds a long stem of grass at one end, then jumps up and down while approaching the female.

HABITAT/RANGE: Occurs along east coast of Australia from south-east South Australia, through Victoria, New South Wales and Queensland.

VOICE: Mournful 'oowee-oowee'.

ESTRILDIDAE

BLACK-THROATED FINCH *Poephila cincta*

SIZE/ID: 10cm. Blue-grey head with black lores and throat. Body cinnamon, tail black and undertail-coverts white.

FOOD/BEHAVIOUR: Both ripe and semi-ripe fruits, berries and grass seeds. Holds grass-stem with foot while removing seeds.

HABITAT/RANGE: Found only in areas of northern Queensland. Prefers habitats where savanna and water prevail.

VOICE: Softly whistled 'tweet-tweet'.

GOULDIAN FINCH *Erythrura gouldiae*

SIZE/ID: 14cm. Rainbow-coloured with green upperparts, yellow belly, purple breast, and blue collar and rump. Crown and cheek can be red, orange or black.

FOOD/BEHAVIOUR: Sorghum and grass seed. Only finch to nest in tree hollows; also uses termite mounds.

HABITAT/RANGE: Occurs in tropical regions of Western Australia, Northern Territory and Queensland. Often seen in flocks in open grasslands.

VOICE: Calls include 'ssitt-ssitt' and variations.

FURTHER READING

Slater, P., Slater, P. and Slater, R. 2009. *The Slater Field Guide to Australian Birds*. Second Edition. Reed New Holland. ISBN 978 1 87706 963 5.

Slater, P. and Elmer, S. 2014. *Glimpses of Australian Birds*. Reed New Holland. ISBN 978 1 92151 742 6.

Van Gessel, F. 2015. *Backyard Bird Sounds*. Reed New Holland. ISBN 978 1 92151 745 7.

GLOSSARY

Adult: an individual which has reached maturity.

Arboreal: living among trees or in them.

Bar: mark across the chest, wings or tail.

Barred: marks cross-ways on body, wings or tail.

Belly: lower part of a bird's underparts, below the breast and flanks

Breeding plumage: term used when birds acquire bright feathers prior to mating.

Call: vocalization produced by a bird to communicate with others.

Camouflage: patterns and/or colours that resemble the surrounding environment.

Cap: the crown of a bird's head.

Cere: a covering of flesh at base of upper part of bill.

Clutch: the group of eggs laid by one female.

Collar: ring of similarly coloured feathers that partly or fully encircle the neck.

Display: body movements

GLOSSARY

to display plumage and communicate.

Diurnal: active during daylight hours.

Endemic: species that is only found in a certain area (often a particular country).

Eye-stripe: narrow strip of feathers that usually runs from bill through eye and beyond.

Flank: side of a bird directly above belly.

Fledgling: young chick which has just left the nest.

Forage: to look for food.

Gape: interior of bird's mouth.

Gibber: hard or stony interior of Australia.

Gizzard: section of the gut where food is stored and ground up before entering the digestion area.

Gliding: flying with out-stretched wings using minimal flaps.

Gregarious: flocking together in large numbers.

Immature: individual which has yet to each breeding age.

Incubate: keeping eggs warm before they hatch.

Juvenile: plumage of a young bird, often immediately after it leaves the nest.

Lobe: decorative flesh protuding from part of a bird, for example on grebes' feet or head of a cassowary.

Mallee: multi-stemmed growth of low eucalypt trees often seen in the semi-arid areas of Australia

Manna: high-energy sugar substance that grows on some eucalypt trees.

Mask: section of dark plumage surrounding the eye.

Migration: flight to another area (often in a different country) for breeding or to spend the winter.

Moult: shedding old feathers and growing new ones.

Nocturnal: active during the night, for example owls.

Nomadic: continually on the move, rarely remaining long in one area.

GLOSSARY

Brood-parasite: bird, such as a cuckoo, which lays its eggs in the nest of another species.

Pelagic: living at sea, only coming to land to nest.

Pellet: a capsule of undigestable food which is regurgitated, for example by owls.

Pied: black and white plumage.

Plumage: the feathers of a bird.

Preening: routine behaviour done by some birds to keep their feathers clean and in good condition.

Range: geographical area where a bird naturally occurs.

Raptor: bird of prey, generally hawks, kites, eagles, falcons and allies.

Saltmarsh: muddy land that is subject to coastal flooding

Scrape: small depression on ground which serves as a nest with very little building-material (by plovers, for example).

Solitary: birds that tend not to mix with other birds or species

Song: loud vocalization often performed by a male to impress a female or drive a rival away from a territory.

Spur: bony growth on leg or wing of some birds, for example Masked Lapwing.

Streak: marks which run lengthways along part of bird.

Supercilium: narrow strip of feathers that usually runs above the eye and eye-stripe.

Talon: sharp hooked claw of a bird of prey.

Territory: area of bush or open land that is controlled by a species for their own use

Vent: area of feathers between legs and base of tail.

Wattle: fleshy lobe attached to a bird's face or neck.

Wingspan: distance from wing-tip to wing-tip when wings spread in a natural fashion.

INDEX

A

Acanthiza chrysorrhoa 153
Acanthiza lineata 154
Acanthiza pusilla 152
Acanthiza reguloides 151
Acrocephalus australis 178
Alectura lathami 30
Alisterus scapularis 102
Anas castanea 25
Anas superciliosa 24
Anhinga novaehollandiae 40
Anseranas semipalmata 16
Anthochaera carunculata 139
Aprosmictus erythropterus 103
Aquila audax 53
Ardea alba 45
Ardea pacifica 42
Ardenna tenuirostris 36
Ardeotis australis 56
Artamus cyanopterus 158
Artamus leucorhynchus 157
Artamus superciliosus 157
Australasian Grebe 31
Australian Brush-turkey 30
Australian Bustard 56
Australian Darter 40
Australian Figbird 167
Australian Gannet 38
Australian Hobby 54
Australian King Parrot 102
Australian Kite 52
Australian Magpie 160
Australian Pelican 41
Australian Pied Oystercatcher 64
Australian Reed-Warbler 178
Australian Ringneck 109
Australian Shelduck 21
Australian White Ibis 48
Australian Wood Duck 23
Aythya australis 26

B

Banded Lapwing 66
Barnardius zonarius 109
Bassian Thrush 181
Biziura lobata 28
Black Swan 20
Black-faced Cuckooshrike 162
Black-fronted Dotterel 68
Black-necked Stork 51
Black-throated Finch 185
Blue-billed Duck 27
Blue-faced Honeyeater 143
Blue-winged Kookaburra 87
Blue-winged Parrot 105
Bourke's Parrot 105
Brolga 61
Brown Thornbill 152
Brown Treecreeper 130
Bubulcus ibis 46
Budgerigar 120
Buff-banded Rail 58
Buff-rumped Thornbill 151
Burhinus grallarius 62
Bush Stone-curlew 62

C

Cacatua galerita 98
Cacatua sanguinea 97
Cacatua tenuirostris 97

Callocephalon fimbriatum 94
Calyptorhynchus banksii 91
Calyptorhynchus funereus 92
Calyptorhynchus latirostris 93
Cape Barren Goose 17
Carnaby's Black Cockatoo 93
Casuarius casuarius 14
Caspian Tern 72
Cattle Egret 46
Cereopsis novaehollandiae 17
Chalcophaps indica 75
Channel-billed Cuckoo 81
Charadrius ruficapillus 67
Chenonetta jubata 23
Chestnut Teal 25
Chlidonias hybrida 74
Chroicocephalus novaehollandiae 70
Cisticola exilis 179
Climacteris picumnus 130
Cockatiel 99
Colluricincla harmonica 163
Columba leucomela 75
Common Bronzewing 76
Coracina novaehollandiae 162
Cormobates leucophaea 129
Corvus mellori 172
Cracticus nigrogularis 160
Cracticus tibicen 160
Cracticus torquatus 159
Crested Pigeon 77
Crimson Chat 144
Crimson Rosella 111
Cyclopsitta diophthalma 119

INDEX

Cygnus atratus 20

D

Dacelo leachii 87
Dacelo novaeguineae 86
Dasyornis broadbenti 147
Dendrocygna arcuata 19
Dendrocygna eytoni 18
Diamond Dove 79
Diamond Firetail 183
Dicaeum hirundinaceum 182
Double-eyed Fig Parrot 119
Dromaius novaehollandiae 15
Ducula bicolor 80
Dusky Moorhen 60
Dusky Woodswallow 158

E

Eastern Barn Owl 82
Eastern Yellow Robin 176
Eastern Yellow-nosed Albatross 34
Eclectus Parrot 104
Eclectus roratus 104
Egretta novaehollandiae 43
Egretta picata 44
Elanus axillaris 52
Elegant Parrot 106
Elseyornis melanops 68
Emerald Dove 75
Emu 15
Entomyzon cyanotis 143
Eolophus roseicapillus 96
Eopsaltria australis 176
Ephippiorhynchus asiaticus 51
Epthianura albifrons 146
Epthianura aurifrons 145
Epthianura tricolor 144

Erythrura gouldiae 185
Eudyptula minor 33
Eurasian Coot 60

F

Fairy Tern 73
Falco cenchroides 55
Falco longipennis 54
Fulica atra 60

G

Galah 96
Gallinula tenebrosa 60
Gallirallus philippensis 58
Gang-gang Cockatoo 94
Geopelia cuneata 79
Geophaps plumifera 78
Glossopsitta concinna 121
Glossopsitta porphyrocephala 123
Glossopsitta pusilla 122
Glycichila melanops 140
Golden Whistler 164
Golden-headed Cisticola 179
Golden-shouldered Parrot 118
Gouldian Finch 185
Grallina cyanoleuca 170
Great Crested Grebe 32
Great Egret 45
Greater Crested Tern 72
Green Rosella 110
Grey Butcherbird 159
Grey Fantail 168
Grey Shrike-thrush 163
Grus rubicunda 61

H

Haematopus longirostris 64
Hardhead 26

Himantopus leucocephalus 63
Hirundapus caudacutus 85
Hirundo neoxena 177
Hooded Plover 69
Hooded Robin 176
Hydroprogne caspia 72

J

Jacky Winter 173

L

Larus pacificus 71
Lathamus discolor 108
Laughing Kookaburra 86
Leipoa ocellata 29
Leucosarcia picata 78
Lichenostomus chrysops 133
Lichenostomus leucotis 135
Lichenostomus melanops 136
Lichenostomus ornatus 137
Lichenostomus virescens 134
Little Corella 97
Little Lorikeet 122
Little Penguin 33
Little Raven 172
Long-billed Corella 97
Lophocroa leadbeateri 95

M

Magpie Goose 16
Magpie-lark 170
Major Mitchell's Cockatoo 95
Malleefowl 29
Malurus cyaneus 131
Manorina melanocephala 138
Masked Lapwing 65
Melanodryas cucullata 176
Meliphaga notata 132

INDEX

Melithreptus lunatus 142
Melopsittacus undulatus 120
Menura novaehollandiae 125
Merops ornatus 90
Microeca fascinans 173
Mistletoebird 182
Morus serrator 38
Musk Duck 28
Musk Lorikeet 121
Myiagra cyanoleuca 171

N

Nankeen Kestrel 55
Nankeen Night-Heron 47
Neochmia temporalis 184
Neophema chrysogaster 107
Neophema chrysostoma 106
Neophema elegans 106
Neophema splendida 108
Neopsephotus bourkii 105
New Holland Honeyeater 141
Ninox novaeseelandiae 83
Noisy Miner 138
Northiella haematogaster 115
Nycticorax caledonicus 47
Nymphicus hollandicus 99

O

Ocyphaps lophotes 77
Olive-backed Oriole 166
Orange Chat 145
Orange-bellied Parrot 107
Oriolus sagittatus 166
Oxyura australis 27

P

Pachycephala pectoralis 164
Pachycephala rufiventris 165
Pacific Black Duck 24

Pacific Gull 71
Painted Buttonquail 57
Pardalotus punctatus 148
Pardalotus striatus 149
Pelagodroma marina 37
Pelecanus conspicillatus 41
Petroica boodang 174
Petroica goodenovii 175
Phalacrocorax varius 39
Phaps chalcoptera 76
Phylidonyris novaehollandiae 141
Pied Butcherbird 160
Pied Cormorant 39
Pied Currawong 161
Pied Heron 44
Pied Imperial-Pigeon 80
Platalea flavipes 50
Platalea regia 50
Platycercus adscitus 114
Platycercus caledonicus 110
Platycercus elegans 111
Platycercus eximius 113
Platycercus icterotis 114
Platycercus venustus 112
Plumed Whistling-Duck 18
Podargus strigoides 84
Podiceps cristatus 32
Poephila cincta 185
Polytelis alexandrae 101
Polytelis anthopeplus 101
Polytelis swainsonii 100
Pomatostomus superciliosus 156
Porphyrio porphyria 59
Princess Parrot 101
Psephotus chrysopterygius 118
Psephotus haematonotus 116

Psephotus varius 117
Ptilonorhynchus maculatus 128
Ptilonorhynchus violaceus 127
Purple Swamphen 59
Purple-crowned Lorikeet 123
Purpureicephalus spurius 119

R

Radjah Shelduck 22
Rainbow Bee-eater 90
Rainbow Lorikeet 124
Red Wattlebird 139
Red-backed Kingfisher 88
Red-browed Finch 184
Red-capped Parrot 119
Red-capped Plover 67
Red-capped Robin 175
Red-tailed Black Cockatoo 91
Red-winged Parrot 103
Regent Bowerbird 126
Regent Parrot 101
Rhipidura albiscapa 168
Rhipidura leucophrys 168
Rhipidura rufifrons 169
Royal Spoonbill 50
Rufous Bristlebird 147
Rufous Fantail 169
Rufous Whistler 165

S

Sacred Kingfisher 89
Satin Bowerbird 127
Satin Flycatcher 171
Scarlet Robin 174
Scarlet-chested Parrot 108
Scythrops novaehollandiae 81
Sericornis frontalis 150
Sericulus chrysocephalus 126

INDEX

Short-tailed Shearwater 36
Shy Albatross 35
Silver Gull 70
Silvereye 180
Singing Honeyeater 134
Smicrornis brevirostris 155
Southern Boobook 83
Southern Cassowary 14
Sphecotheres vieilloti 167
Spinifex Pigeon 78
Spotted Bowerbird 128
Spotted Pardalote 148
Stagonopleura guttata 183
Sternula nereis 73
Straw-necked Ibis 49
Strepera graculina 161
Striated Pardalote 149
Striated Thornbill 154
Sulphur-crested Cockatoo 98
Superb Fairy-wren 131
Superb Lyrebird 125
Superb Parrot 100
Swift Parrot 108

T

Tachybaptus novaehollandiae 31
Tadorna radjah 22
Tadorna tadornoides 21
Tawny Frogmouth 84
Tawny-crowned Honeyeater 140

Thalassarche carteri 34
Thalassarche cauta 35
Thalasseus bergii 72
Thinornis rubricollis 69
Threskiornis molucca 48
Threskiornis spinicollis 49
Todiramphus pyrrhopygius 88
Todiramphus sanctus 89
Trichoglossus haematodus 124
Turnix varius 57
Tyto delicatula 82

V

Vanellus miles 65
Vanellus tricolor 66

W

Wandering Whistling-Duck 19
Wedge-tailed Eagle 53
Weebill 155
Welcome Swallow 177
Whiskered Tern 74
White-breasted Woodswallow 157
White-browed Babbler 156
White-browed Scrubwren 150
White-browed Woodswallow 157

White-eared Honeyeater 135
White-faced Heron 43
White-faced Storm-Petrel 37
White-fronted Chat 146
White-headed Pigeon 75
White-headed Stilt 63
White-naped Honeyeater 142
White-necked Heron 42
White-throated Needletail 85
White-throated Treecreeper 129
Willie-wagtail 168
Wonga Pigeon 78

Y

Yellow-billed Spoonbill 50
Yellow-faced Honeyeater 133
Yellow-plumed Honeyeater 137
Yellow-rumped Thornbill 153
Yellow-spotted Honeyeater 132
Yellow-tailed Black Cockatoo 92
Yellow-tufted Honeyeater 136

Z

Zoothera lunulata 181
Zosterops lateralis 180

OTHER TITLES IN THE SERIES

Reed Concise Guide: Animals of Australia (ISBN 978 1 92151 754 9)
Reed Concise Guide: Wildflowers of Australia (ISBN 978 1 92151 755 6)